THE ONLY
AXOLOTL
CARE GUIDE
YOU'LL EVER NEED

WRITTEN BY
GEORGE FERON

Avoid Deadly Mistakes & Learn from a Pro:
Everything You Need to Know to Raise Healthy and
Happy Axolotls *in Your Own Home*

TABLE OF CONTENTS

CHAPTER 1

The Graceful Axolotl

CHAPTER 2

All About Housing Axolotls

CHAPTER 3
Feeding Your Axolotls

CHAPTER 4

Health Issues With Axolotls

CHAPTER 5

All About Breeding Axolotls

CHAPTER 6

Morphed Axolotls

INTRODUCTION

"There was a time when I thought a great deal about the axolotls. I went to see them in the aquarium at the Jardin des Plantes and stayed for hours watching them, observing their immobility, their faint movements. Now I am an axolotl."

— "Axolotl," by Julio Cortázar

AXOLOTLS ARE ADORABLE animals, so it's common for someone with aquariums to walk into a fish store, see that cute little animal standing at the bottom of a tank, and impulsively buy it. They take it home and place it in a tropical aquarium. After a while, they start noticing that small fish are gone, and the axolotl is demonstrating strange behavior: always hiding, frightened, or floating close to the water's surface. Later, they find out that their little amphibian has been eating the gravel they used as a substrate, and then the axolotl suddenly stops eating and pooping. In the end, the animal dies, and this individual swears never to keep one of these salamanders again, as they are sensitive aquatic animals.

Unfortunately, this is something that most of us have gone through, either as uninformed hobbyists or even more informed ones who decided to take home an animal they didn't know very well, believing that everything would work out. As strange and irresponsible as it may be, these mistakes are part of everyone's learning, and teach us to do it right in the future.

If the keeper described above had researched a little more, they would have known some main points in the maintenance of these animals, such as the fact that axolotls live in cold water, are predators, and that you should never use gravel as a substrate in their aquariums. With the growing popularity of these animals, through their representation in games and on various social media platforms, they seem to many to be super resistant and easy-to-care-for animals, who do not need special care. But that is not the case.

I will always remember my first axolotl. I was just a 14-year-old kid, always looking for strange animals to keep in my aquariums and terrariums; the first time I saw one of these salamanders, it was love at first sight. I asked the store owner how to keep them, and then I brought him home. With a lot of effort, I set up an aquarium with a filter and everything else I thought it needed. That's when the problems started. At first, I didn't understand why it stood at the bottom of the aquarium without moving. I thought something was wrong. But after seeing the animal feed properly, I imagined it was something specific to that individual. Then I noticed some pebbles of gravel came out in its poop; that's when I decided to remove all the substrate, but this caused an ammonia spike in my aquarium.

After all the work and numerous water changes, I managed to normalize the tank, but then came summer. Unfortunately, it was a hot German summer, which began a saga of stress for my young axolotl and also for me, its young owner. The freezer in my house was always full of frozen bottles and ice cubes. I spent minutes, hours, and days looking at the thermometer to try to control and stabilize the temperature of the water, always without success. I even resorted to putting the animal inside the fridge. It was then that a fungus attacked him and took his life.

All this work and suffering made me extremely frustrated, and it took me several years to decide to keep another axolotl. But on the other hand, it made me exhaustively prepare myself through research, reading, and talking with keepers and breeders. This is how I managed to become a successful axolotl owner and breeder. To this day, I keep countless creatures from my first pair of these salamanders; they all live happily and are well cared for, and I possess that pride that only hobbyists know and understand.

Shouldn't we all always walk this path of keeping animals responsibly? Every hobbyist should always research the animal, its behavior and needs, and, in addition, determine whether or not it fits your lifestyle and financial situation. And maybe you've even given up on keeping axolotls because no matter how much you've read and researched, you couldn't make it happen the right way. Well, there's a lot of information out there, but that doesn't mean it's correct or written by someone with first-hand experience.

Some have even bought books and received coaching from "renowned keepers." But take note: these "keepers" don't really care about animals and just want to make money from unsuspecting hobbyists. Regardless of your previous knowledge or age, I wrote this book to present to you the wealth of information and techniques I have learned throughout my trajectory as a successful hobby-ist, so you can change your perception of axolotls and be able to care for them in the right way.

In this book you will find information about this graceful animal, its maintenance needs, how to feed and care for it correctly, its major diseases, reproduction, and even an entire chapter dedicated to its metamorphosis. I got here the hard way but now am able to pass on my life's work and knowledge to you. Just because my first experience with these animals was difficult doesn't mean yours has to be. Get ready to learn the best way to deal with these beautiful amphibians. Allow me to guide you through this exciting journey.

Let's begin!

How To Get The Most Out Of This Book

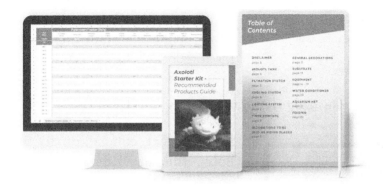

To help you along your journey, we've created a set of free bonuses that includes an Axolotl Starter Kit, Daily/Weekly Axolotl Care Logbook, and more to help you get the best possible results. These files will be mentioned in the relevant chapters.

We highly recommend you sign up now to get the most out of this book. You can do that by going to the link below.

breakfreepublications.com/axolotl-bonus

Free Bonus #1 Axolotl Starter Kit: Recommended Products

Here you will find the list of all the essential products hand-picked by our team of experts so that you can confidently care for your axolotls and maintain their habitat at its best.

Free Bonus #2 Daily/ Weekly Axolotl Care Log

As a perfect companion to this Book, this user-friendly Google spreadsheet empowers you to monitor and record crucial parameters in your axolotl aquarium on a Daily or Weekly basis.

Free Bonus #3 Free Audiobook Version of the book

For a limited time, and as a "Thank you" for purchasing this book, you are eligible for the audio version of our Axolotl Care Guide. After signing up, you will get a private link to access the Audiobook.

To get your bonuses, go to
breakfreepublications.com/axolotl-bonus

CHAPTER 1
THE GRACEFUL AXOLOTL

THE AXOLOTL, ALSO known as the Mexican salamander, is an amphibian with the scientific name Ambystoma mexicanum. Initially found in Mexico, the animal became known worldwide in 1864 after the first species found were taken to Paris. After that, Europeans began cultivating this amphibian, which reproduces quickly in captivity.

In its natural environment, the axolotl is mainly found in dark colors, ranging from brown to black. Other colorations, such as a pinkish or white appearance, are the result of breeding and selection in captivity. Unfortunately, few specimens are found in the wild. Capture for illegal trade and food, along with the loss of habitat, are factors that contributed to their critically endangered status, according to the IUCN (International Union for the Conservation of Nature).

Axolotls are freshwater aquatic animals with gills, webbed feet, dorsal fins, and a tail. This creature is carnivorous, with a diet consisting of small fish, mollusks, tadpoles, arthropods, fish eggs, zooplankton, and terrestrial larvae. These amphibians are pretty peculiar. They live in dark and freshwater environments, they have three pairs of external gills, and, most amazingly, they have a high regenerative capacity. In addition, they spend their entire life in the larval stage, although they are capable of reproduction.

Axolotls do not undergo the process of metamorphosis, which is common in other amphibians — in which animals develop lungs and legs to walk on the surface. Instead, an axolotl is a neotenic animal, or a species that maintains its larval characteristics even after reaching the adult stage. It maintains this larval and juvenile state throughout its life.

These amphibians are endemic to Mexico, specifically Lake Xochimilco and its surroundings, and measure approximately 25 centimeters in length. The axolotl is closely linked to the native culture of the Mexicans, being part of local mythology. An Aztec legend says that the axolotl embodies the Mayan god of fire and lightning, Xolotl, Quetzalcóatl's twin brother. To avoid being sacrificed, Xolotl took the form of this extraordinary amphibian. He is described as a god with the skeleton of a man and the head of a monster. No wonder his figure is reminiscent of an aquatic salamander with external gills.

They can live for about twelve years, reaching sexual maturity about twelve months after birth, between June and December, or in captivity, when a sudden decrease in temperature is promoted. When breeding, the male deposits his sperm in a pouch, which the female collects through her cloacal opening. It spawns on rocks and leaves approximately one day after this event. The larvae hatch about two weeks later and are approximately a centimeter long. Salamanders are the only vertebrate animals that can regenerate body parts, something that has been catching the attention of scientists for decades.

This ability is even more evident in axolotls, as they can recover extensive structures without leaving a scar in the area. In addition to regenerating limbs, the animal can rebuild its entire spinal cord! This has enormous potential in scientific research because it can help advance areas like tissue regeneration and recovery of function.

Morphs

Since axolotls have been widely bred in captivity for more than 150 years, numerous breeders have been selecting and improving individuals, obtaining different colors and patterns. As a result, we currently find around 20 morphs (varieties) on the market, and new ones are constantly being created. Each variety has its name and classification, which can often be complicated for those outside the Axolotl community to understand. Breeders assign these names, which are then adopted by the community. Each morph is created by breeding and selecting specific individuals with the traits desired by the breeder. Each has a degree of rarity, directly dictating its market value. Varieties such as albino and leucistic are considered standards, easily obtainable, and always affordable. However, nowadays, morphs like 'Firefly' and 'Enigma' are rare and can reach incredibly high values.

Stages of life

Now that you know a little about this creature, we can talk about its life cycle. This salamander begins its life as a tiny egg. In nature, you can find these animals submerged at considerable depth near the banks of rivers where the current is not very strong. Once out of the egg, the little pale tadpoles live in calm pools on the shores of lakes.

After a while, the axolotl develops limbs that will allow it to move on land. However, unlike its relatives, it will never lose its gills or dorsal fin as it grows. In the larval stage, the axolotl has a broad head with pinkish gill tufts, large eyes, and an elongated and laterally flattened body, slightly longer than the tail, which is compressed and bears a dorsal crest.

The axolotl's complete life cycle is carried out within the aquatic environment. Its average lifespan is 15 years in the wild, but in captivity, it can live anywhere from 25 to 30 years. The egg is the first stage in its development. It measures approximately two millimeters and is protected by a gelatinous substance produced by the mother's segregation and her contact with water. The embryo will originate after a week and will measure about 11 millimeters. After another week, the egg will hatch, and the third phase will begin.

In the larval stage, the body becomes transparent due to the lack of skin cells, so we can see the animal's internal organs and digestive processes. First, it develops the forelimbs and, a week later, the hind limbs. At this stage, the larva will be between 11 and 50 millimeters. The final stage, i.e., adult, will begin a few weeks after the limbs originate; however, it will not be a full adult until around 18 months or two years. The standard measurement of mature wild adults is usually between 23 and 25 centimeters. Although the size depends on the animal's environment, condition, and diet, it can grow up to 40 centimeters in captivity.

What makes axolotls unique?

The ability to regenerate is the most incredible and unique feature that we find in these animals. The axolotl is the only vertebrate animal capable of fully regenerating itself. Since its discovery by modern science, this feature has attracted scientists' attention. This salamander can regenerate limbs, tissues, and even organs of its body. Axolotls can restore amputated limbs quickly; in just a few weeks, the regeneration is complete, and tissues, cartilage, nerves, muscles, and everything else grow just as before. The only difference is that some eccentricities can occur in this new growth, for example, an extra finger. But that is something to be expected in such a remarkable trait.

Its regenerative ability is so unique that it can even regenerate damage to its nervous system, such as deep wounds to the spinal cord, renewing it to the point where it seems as if no damage has ever occurred. Add to that any injury, from the retina to a simple superficial wound, all without leaving any scar.

Another characteristic noticed since this animal was first taken to Europe is its ease of reproducing in captivity. This fact allows scientists, who can create a practically infinite stock, to research the incredible characteristics of this species and uncover its mysteries.

The study of the species is vital to learning how the different processes related to the regeneration and repair of various tissues can be applied in human medicine. Just imagine, one day, with the help of these small animals, we can repair severe neurological damage, helping people to walk again. Incredible! Through genetic sequencing, scientists have discovered that the axolotl has the largest genome ever seen to date - ten times larger than the base pairs of human DNA; these salamanders have 32 billion base pairs of DNA, while humans have only three billion! Researchers believe that in this DNA is contained the secret of this super-regeneration.

These animals are so unique that they even have different breathing methods. As they are entirely aquatic animals, they can obtain oxygen from the water through their gills and skin; despite this, they can breathe atmospheric air through their rudimentary lungs. It was once thought that the axolotl is a primitive animal because, until recently, it was believed that amphibians with gills were the oldest animals. However, several fossils have indicated that the gill apparatus disappeared as an animal matured, as in the case of current batrachians (frogs, toads, and treefrogs), so the axolotl is no longer considered to be a living fossil but a well-evolved species that presents different characteristics from most of the others that exist.

Conservation

As it is a critically endangered species, several conservation programs are underway and it is also a protected species. These animals live in Mexico City, home to one of the most emblematic ecosystems of high social and biological value; the Xochimilco and San Gregorio Atlapulco Lake System is a protected natural area and is on the list of wetlands of world importance. In addition, UNESCO declared this area a World Heritage Site along with the Historic Center of Mexico City on December 11, 1987.

Currently, the Xochimilco Lake region faces several socio-environmental problems that have led to its deterioration: the springs that fed it have dried up, and its channels are contaminated by wastewater discharges and excessive use of insecticides and chemical fertilizers in agricultural production. Unfortunately, urban sprawl is also constantly growing.

Among the axolotl conservation plans is, for example, the in situ (in the natural habitat) work of the chinampa refuge in Xochimilco, promoting isolated channels and water with a higher degree of cleanliness and quality. At the same time, we see ex situ (outside the natural habitat) work like that done by the University of Mexico, where a temporary refuge is granted to these animals.

For the conservation of this species, we see more and more projects being developed by civil and academic institutions, with numerous initiatives. Among these is the implementation of a Biological Production and Conservation Center, where the study, conservation, and propagation of native flora and fauna species is developed. It also supports the rehabilitation and preservation of the wetland through reforestation and biological monitoring.

Axolotls as gods

As it is an endemic species of Mexico, specifically the ancient lakes of the Valley of Mexico, the axolotl's history is linked to the cultures that inhabited the region, such as the Mexicas, who considered it a god. One legend says that long ago, the gods decided to meet in Teotihuacan to create the universe by offering their own lives in sacrifice. Deities such as Huitzilopochtli, Xochipilli, and Tezcatlipoca, among others, threw themselves into the fire; however, one of them did not want to do so because he was afraid. This was Xolotl, the dog god and twin of Quetzalcóatl.

Although his immolation was essential to give motion to the stars and thus complete the invention of the universe, Xolotl did not want to burn. So he quickly fled from Teotihuacan to an unknown destination. The gods were angry, and ordered the Wind to find him so the sacrifice could be fulfilled. However, the task took work, as Xolotl began to transform into various species so he could not be found.

The first form he adopted was that of a turkey, but when the proximity of the Wind threatened him, he became maguey (a type of native plant). He then took the form of a Xoloitzcuintle dog but was tracked down again, so he altered his body to look like a corn plant. Despite all the transformations, Xolotl was located by the envoy of the gods. Having no escape, he decided to throw himself into the lake, transforming himself into an axolotl.

Xolotl's new appearance was that of a small amphibian with horn-shaped gills that helped him breathe in water. He sailed for days inside the lake, saving his life until the Wind finally caught him. He was taken back to Teotihuacan to finish the ritual, and the stars began to move with the first drop of his blood that fell. Thus, the gods completed the creation of the universe.

Fun facts

With their distinctive appearance and diverse colors, these animals seem to have come from a peaceful world, with their apparent smile and facial features that delight everyone who sees them. Let's review all we've just learned about these beautiful creatures.

- The name axolotl comes from the Nahuatl Axolotl, which means 'water monster,' and has been known since the time of the Aztecs.

- It is an animal with a strong connection to local mythology. It is related to the god Xólotl, twin brother of Quetzalcóatl, who refused to self-sacrifice and escaped, finally transforming into an axolotl and entering the water.

- The axolotl is not like the frog's tadpole. It is a salamander that, unlike other amphibians, does not undergo metamorphosis. It is a neotenic species that can reach sexual maturity without losing its larval characteristics.

- It is the only animal capable of regenerating any part of its body in days or weeks, leaving no traces or scars. It can regenerate limbs, including bones, jaw, skin, organs, spine, retina, brain, and heart.

- The axolotl does not have eyelids. Its body has three pairs of gills that allow it to breathe underwater and it has a fin that goes from just below its head to its tail.

- On the front legs, they have only four toes, while on the hind legs, they have five.

- For each mating, a mother axolotl lays between 300 and 1,000 eggs of a jelly-like consistency. Babies are born with a tail, gills, and two structures on either side of the head to attach themselves to the environment.

- The axolotl's only habitat is water. These animals spend their entire lives underwater. They breathe like fish through their gills and skin structures that absorb oxygen from the water and have rudimentary lungs that can breathe atmospheric air.

- Axolotls have a cartilaginous skeleton that never calcifies, even in old age. Their muscles are like those of fish, indicating their aquatic evolutionary origin. Their teeth and strong jaw allow them to firmly grab their prey and destroy it before it passes into the digestive system.

- The color of axolotls is very diverse. They can be black, but they are also brown, white, and even albino, without skin pigmentation.

- Recently, these amphibians have gained tremendous popularity, and one of the main reasons for this is the game *Minecraft*.

Axolotls in *Minecraft*

In June 2021, a viral computer game called *Minecraft* included an axolotl in its update, which was promptly a success. Because of this hit, the search for them in the real world has exploded, especially among children and young people. Still, adults were not left out, creating a frenzy of impulsive purchases by those who had never actually seen this lovely amphibian.

Although the animal in the game appears to have some similarities with real life, in practice, keeping something virtual is very different from doing so in the physical world, so this has led to maintenance failures and animal suffering. Here I must reiterate that *no one should ever purchase an animal impulsively*. Before going after the pet, you should always research and obtain as much information as possible. Bringing your new pet home is the last step for anyone who wants to keep these animals properly.

When we compare the animal in *Minecraft* with the one we find in our aquariums and stores, we can see more differences than similarities. And even though *Minecraft* has a care guide for axolotls, you should never use it with real animals! In the game, the rarest color found is blue; in the real world, you can see this color doesn't even exist. The rarest are those that mix more than one color, such as 'Firefly,' 'Enigma,' and 'Chimera.'

One feature that helped with gameplay is that, in the *Minecraft* universe, axolotls can live out of water for a few minutes. In the real world, this does not happen, as these amphibians spend their entire lives in the water. It's also pretty weird that they can live in salt water in the virtual world and are found in the ocean, which makes no sense; ideally, they should live at 0 salinity, even if they can withstand a condition of around 15 percent salinity. They are also easily located in the game, which differs remarkably from reality, as they are rare and difficult to find animals.

In terms of food, *Minecraft* comes close. In the game, they feed on tropical fish, which occurs in both captive and wild axolotls. But these animals eat a much more diverse diet, and small live fish are just a tiny part of their diet. The game also almost succeeded in reproducing the animal's regenerative factor. However, in reality, these animals regenerate slower than those portrayed in the game, in addition to being able to regenerate limbs with some weird consequences, like an extra finger.

As for behavior, these animals are the complete opposite of what the game presents. In *Minecraft*, they are active, light animals that perform various activities; in the real world, they are the opposite. Axolotls are incredibly sedentary animals that spend hours immobile at the bottom of the aquarium. One feature they hit the nail on is that these animals are lovely and graceful. This no one can deny.

Keeping axolotls as pets

A prevalent mistake that usually leads to the early death of axolotls is the belief that they don't need much care. Although it is true that the axolotl is not prone to illness, it is imperative to have a well-structured aquarium, with all factors controlled, and that you are aware of the special care necessary to maintain this animal.

Before bringing your axolotl into your home, ensure you have everything the animal needs. A good-sized aquarium with a sound filtration system, properly cycled, with temperature controls and gauges. Remember that axolotls need cold water to be healthy and live well.

The aquarium must be of a significant size (axolotls like to move over all available surfaces), with hiding places for them, and preferably include live plants. A minimum of 40-50 liters (approximately 10.5-13 gallons) of water is required for each juvenile animal; for an adult, use an aquarium of at least 150 to 200 liters (approximately 40-53 gallons). The tank must be adequately supported and level on its stand or furniture; in this way, accidents are avoided.

Depending on your filtration system, it is ideal to use an aerator (air pump) as a complement, offering an adequate amount of oxygen so the axolotl can breathe comfortably with its gills. A significant factor for the maintenance of these animals is the temperature (15-18°C, or 59-64.4°F), so, depending on the region where you live, it is necessary to use a chiller-type cooler. The chiller is probably the most expensive item in an axolotl aquarium, but it is the most important.

If the water is too warm, these amphibians are predisposed to stress, infections, and other diseases, and may also complete the metamorphosis by reaching the surface and dying shortly afterward. The danger is greatest in summer when high temperatures can cause aquarium water to reach over 25°C (77° F). It has been well established that more rudimentary cooling methods, such as submerging frozen water bottles, aerators, and fans, do not result in an adequate cooling effect.

The water temperature for adults mustn't exceed 22°C (71.6°F). Newborn axolotls need a water temperature between 22 and 24°C, and shouldn't exceed 25°C. Temperatures should be progressively reduced for juveniles at a rate of 1°C (33.8°F) every 2-3 days. A good filter is essential to maintain water quality and prevent the buildup of harmful substances, such as ammonia and nitrites. Ensure the filter and aquarium are properly cycled and the filter power is sufficient for the size of the aquarium.

Equally essential is your weekly dedication to cleaning and maintaining the aquarium, eliminating waste and excrement and maintaining optimal water and environmental quality. Finally, it is crucial to arrange the filter so it does not create a strong current, which will stress your amphibian.

Maintenance is not time-consuming or exhausting, but it is vital for all who maintain aquariums. It must be carried out in a specific way, and includes several important tasks, such as cleaning the substrate, decorations, and water change. Therefore, maintenance equipment, such as siphons, hoses, and buckets, is very important.

Live plants, in addition to creating a more natural look, can help control the level of nitrates and oxygenate the water. They also serve as a hiding place. The Java fern (Microsorum Pteropus) is a simple and easy-care plant that adapts well to water temperatures of 18-19°C (64.4-66.2°F). Also, moss balls (Cladophora Aegagropila) grow well and are good oxygenating agents.

Axolotls feed by forcefully sucking food. The aquarium substrate should never consist of stones that fit in the large mouth of the animal, as well as other materials that they can swallow; this is one of the biggest causes of death for these animals. Light sandy substrates that are fine enough that, if ingested, do not pose a health risk are best.

Other care, like conditioning the water to be placed in the aquarium when replenishing, is necessary. Use suitable conditioners that eliminate chlorine, chloramines, and other toxic substances. Chlorine is harmful to axolotls and nitrifying bacteria (essential for correct biological filtration).

Maintaining the pH between 6.5 and 8 is also necessary, as is ensuring the hardness of the water does not drop too much. Ammonia and other nitrogenous compounds should be undetectable in a well-cycled aquarium with proper filter maintenance. Always have a specialized test kit for freshwater aquariums to carry out measurements.

Remember that these animals are amphibians with bare skin covered with mucus, so they are extremely sensitive to their environment, so the quality of both the water and the aquarium must always be impeccable. Axolotls that are kept in perfect condition and without stress are rarely prone to disease or other ailments and thrive.

Costs of keeping an axolotl

To keep these pets, you must think long-term. As they are animals that live an incredible length of time in captivity (there are reports of axolotls over 20 years old!), you must ensure that you have all the financial and social conditions necessary to provide all the animal needs throughout its life. Fortunately, axolotls are not expensive to purchase or maintain.

The most common morphs can be bought for less than $50, unlike rarer varieties that cost more than $1,000. In addition, you have the initial cost of equipment; this value can vary, depending on the material and brand of aquarium and equipment, but starting at around $420, you can put together a great setup that will last a long time.

In addition to the initial cost, however, you must also consider the monthly cost of keeping these animals. There are several considerations with regard to monthly cost: the food, the energy used by the equipment, and eventually, you'll have to buy things like new test kits and water conditioner. The values of these things differ significantly but it's best to budget around $120 per month, as food must be based on live food, which costs a little more than industrialized foods. You may also incur occasional costs like veterinary care, which can be quite expensive. Be sure to research specialized veterinarians in your region and their costs before bringing home this lovely little animal.

Feeding

Axolotls are predators. In the wild, they consume a wide variety of prey, such as copepods, insect larvae, small fish, and crustaceans. In captivity, we must also offer them a varied diet. They accept many invertebrates in their diet, and when larger, they can also eat small fish. A good and practical option is to use frozen foods.

For young axolotls, we can resort to frozen freshwater fish (bloodworms or mosquito larvae, Daphnia, brine shrimp, or Tubifex). For larger specimens, we can feed them small, low-fat fish, such as some livebearers, which can also be frozen. Using small fish that the axolotl can consume whole (or chopped) with skin, skeleton, and viscera is essential.

You should not use fatty fish or fish with rigid bones (anchovies, sardines, etc.). Finally, they can eat live fish, such as guppies, endlers, or the like. However, this is an option that many axolotl owners feel bad about and is also more expensive. Fish fillets should not be fed to axolotls, as their diet would be incomplete. For the same reason, we should not provide them with meat. The ideal is always to use live food and to be prepared to deal with earthworms, Tubifex, and live bloodworms. Many axolotls also accept insects like cockroaches, crickets, and mealworms.

Newborn axolotls are quite herbivorous in their first 24-48 hours. In the first hours of life, axolotl larvae still feed on yolk remains, but they will quickly need microalgae, such as spirulina, to survive. Therefore, after 24 hours, we should offer them live invertebrates of no more than three millimeters, such as Daphnia (water flea). You can also use Artemia salina nauplii (brine shrimp), but it is more work because, unlike Daphnia, it must be filtered and washed to avoid excess salt. After 48 hours, other options are fine, such as the small Tubifex. Later, frozen and more significant foods are gradually introduced.

Behavior

Because they are nocturnal animals, axolotls tend to be more active at night or when they perceive little light in their environment. In addition, they are solitary and sedentary animals, spending most of their time stationary at the bottom of the aquarium, but this changes at feeding time, when they move more and may even chase the food offered.

Be alert if your axolotl spends much time on the surface. Ensure it's not stressed or sick, and check the water parameters. Above all, remember that they are susceptible to stress. You may also see them moving the substrate and plants in the aquarium from side to side. This is an interesting behavior to watch and appears beneficial for the animal.

While adapting to their new aquarium, or when they feel uncomfortable for some reason, they tend to hide, displaying timid behavior. However, with time and the right conditions in the aquarium, they become more confident and spend time in the most visible parts. Also, after getting used to you, they might swim close when they see you (expecting to be fed, of course).

Young specimens are more restless, swim non-stop, and may even fight at mealtimes. However, as time passes, they become calmer and less aggressive toward each other. These salamanders generally remain almost inactive during the day, coming to the surface of the water sporadically to breathe. Then, at dusk, they come out of their lethargy and start looking for food.

Axolotls communicate through chemical and visual signals, but this mainly occurs during mating season. Another form of communication is through pheromones, also during the reproductive phase. They capture their prey thanks to their ability to identify electrical fields and by detecting chemical signals.

Metamorphosis

Amphibians were the first vertebrates to jump from water to land. However, unlike most amphibians, the axolotl does not usually complete its metamorphosis, but is instead a salamander with a larval aspect even in the adult stage (what is known as neoteny).

But in some cases (mainly triggered by stress), they can undergo a metamorphosis that leads them to become salamanders. However, it is a very stressful process, and its life in the Earth phase is very short. So this is not desirable.

Metamorphosis is a natural process in many amphibians, and is influenced by several environmental factors. Temperature, for example, affects their endocrine system, which is responsible for the production of thyroxine (T4), a hormone that acts on the metabolism of cells to carry out the development and growth processes. It also induces changes in the levels of thyroid hormone receptors, as well as the enzymes responsible for metabolizing it, and when high levels of T4 occur, metamorphosis is activated.

Neotenic species have an insufficient plasma concentration of T4, which determines a low rate of thyroid-stimulating hormone (TSH) secretion. This, in turn, blocks the metamorphic change that organisms must undergo. However, this does not influence their reproductive maturity.

In captivity, metamorphosis can be forced through stress by environmental factors or even through hormones injected into the animal, but the physiological pressure is very high. Metamorphosed animals usually have difficulty feeding and live for a short time, rarely exceeding one to two years of life.

Legality

Though they are scarce in the wild, these animals are increasingly bred in captivity. Because they have been bred in captivity for so many years, they are both genetically and morphologically distant from those that inhabit Lake Xochimilco. Incredible research (Woodcock et al., 2017) points out that all axolotls on the market today are hybrid populations, crossed by breeders from 1967 onwards with the tiger salamander (Ambystoma tigrinum). In addition to being kept in laboratories for studies, axolotls are now being bred in aquariums by those who enjoy maintaining aquariums, amphibians and aquatic animals.

Each state in the United States has a specific law regulating the maintenance, sale, and importation of axolotls.

For example, these animals are prohibited in California, Maine, and New Jersey. Hawaii and New Mexico have regulations that say you must have a permit to keep them in captivity. In New Mexico, it is even forbidden to import them. The prohibition and regulation of these animals' maintenance, trade, and import go beyond the US. They are considered legal animals in Canada but prohibited in New Brunswick, British Columbia, Winnipeg, and Prince Edward Island. In Nova Scotia, possession and trade are regulated. You need a CITES (Convention on International Trade in Endangered Species) permit to keep it.

In European countries, it is a little more complicated, as there are laws within the European Union and individual laws in each country. Generally speaking, they are legal to keep as long as you have a CITES license, which regulates the trade of endangered exotic animal species, and you obtain your axolotl from countries within the EU. Always consult the responsible body in your country before purchasing these animals.

These restrictions exist for several reasons. The main one is that axolotls are critically endangered animals, so trade regulation helps maintain the population of wild animals, stimulating their reproduction in captivity and inhibiting the collection and sale of illegal individuals. Another reason is that these amphibians could be a potential invader species, destabilizing native populations of other salamanders and aquatic animals and passing on previously non-existent diseases to wild populations.

Pros and cons of keeping an axolotl

Axolotls have become very fashionable in recent years. They are great pets, easy to keep, and interact with their owners, even though they must always be in the aquatic environment. Above all, they are exceptionally lovable, peaceful and charming animals with curious and endearing behavior.

At the same time, they are critically endangered animals in their natural environment, with the potential to be invasive in other environments, and need a very specific setup, since they are easily stressed, which can cause them to die prematurely.

But with some knowledge about the species and its habits, these problems can be overcome. If you're sure that keeping an axolotl as a pet is the perfect choice for you and suits your circumstances and lifestyle, it's time to learn more about these beautiful animals.

CHAPTER 2

ALL ABOUT HOUSING AXOLOTLS

D URING THE FIRST chapter of this book, we talked about what this wonderful animal is and where it comes from. This information is necessary to determine if this pet is right for you. If keeping an axolotl fits perfectly into your lifestyle and you're able to meet the needs of the animal, continue reading to learn how to keep these cute animals without any problems.

Before you bring home an axolotl

As mentioned earlier, axolotls spend their entire lives in the water, so we must provide an aquatic environment for these animals. In addition, they are sensitive animals when it comes to their environment. This is one of the reasons they are in danger of extinction, so we must create a fully controlled environment. Before legally and ethically obtaining your salamander, you must have the entire aquarium ready and stable to accommodate them.

Get your supplies

To start, you will need the basics to set up a cold water aquarium: the container, a cooler system, filter, and meters. You should have:

- A container of at least 120 liters (32 gallons). The material does not matter, but glass or acrylic is usually used;

- Filtration system: An essential part, you must have at least biological media (something that provides extra surface area for bacteria to grow, like ceramic rings or bio-balls). It is also advisable to have activated carbon to prevent strong smells. Also, the filter pump should not create a strong flow of water;

- Cooling system: The most efficient cooling systems are chiller-type systems, but some breeders use automated coolers with controllers;

- Lighting system: Axolotls do not like bright environments but must receive a minimum of light to differentiate day and night.

To compose the internal part of the aquarium, we use:

- Decorations to serve as hiding places. For example, caves designed for this purpose;

- General decorations, like rocks, and live or artificial plants. In addition to the aesthetic improvement, this will create a more favorable place for your pet;

- Substrate: Always use the finest sand possible, or do not use any substrate (bare bottom).

Maintenance equipment is needed, such as:

- Siphon, bucket, and hoses. These help with cleaning and water changes;

- Sponges, to clean glass and decorations. You should only use the sponge in the aquarium and without chemical products;

- Thermometer and water test kit: These devices are crucial to keep you informed about what's happening with the water in your aquarium.

- Long tweezers. Tweezers help a lot when feeding your pet.

- Water conditioner prepares the water for your aquarium, removing chloramine and other toxic compounds.

- Aquarium net.

Avoid products, even well-known brands, that contain chemicals like iodine or other substances. Axolotls have bare skin without protection, so these products are highly toxic to these animals.

If in doubt, check freebie bonus #1 Axolotl Starter kit; there, you will find the list of all the essential products hand-picked by our team of experts.

Setting up your aquarium

Installation of equipment is generally effortless. But when choosing these items, you will need to keep in mind the size of the aquarium, as the equipment's excellent performance and the axolotl's comfort are directly related to the amount of water that will need to be filtered and oxygenated. In addition, alternating periods of light and shade are crucial for your axolotl's well-being, so the choice of the light fixture should suit the width, length, and depth of the aquarium.

The cooling system is the most complicated piece of equipment. I strongly recommend using chillers. Fan-type coolers can do the job but are less efficient because they require different systems, like controllers and probes, and can cause temperature fluctuations. The beginner aquarist must look for a reliable store and ask the seller or shopkeeper questions. These people will always be willing to collaborate with you, and this will help establish a bond and clear out any doubts you may have.

If you prefer, you can also buy a complete aquarium, which comes with all these items already installed. It is usually a little more expensive than purchasing the equipment separately, but not only will it save you time but you may find it more practical. It is also advisable that the aquarist research a lot before beginning the assembly process.

One tip: although many people think that taking care of a smaller aquarium is much easier, the truth is that maintaining the parameters of the water in these aquariums can be a challenge, because in less water, an imbalance can occur more quickly and therefore require more maintenance. And when your pet grows, you'll have to find a bigger place for it anyway. If you still opt for a small aquarium, remember that you must strictly control the water parameters.

Tank size

As we've learned, these amphibians are fully aquatic animals. While it may occasionally come to the surface of the water to breathe with its rudimentary lungs, a healthy specimen never needs to leave the water. And even though they are sedentary animals, they end up standing in different corners of the aquarium, so they need a spacious environment. Horizontal space is arguably more important than vertical space. For the height of the water column, something around 20 cm (about 7.9 inches) is optimal for these animals.

Since an axolotl can easily reach 30 cm (nearly 12 inches) in good conditions, choosing an aquarium with around 100 to 120 liters is advisable. The bigger the aquarium - in addition to being easier to keep the parameters stable - the better your salamander will grow and the better quality of life it will have. The size of the aquarium will also have a direct relationship to the decorations you choose. No matter how many decorations, hiding places, and plants you want in your tank, it's essential always to keep ample space for your pet to swim, explore and rest freely.

Axolotls produce a lot of waste, so you must have a good amount of water and keep up to date with its maintenance. If you want to keep more than one of these animals, ensure they are the same size (to prevent cannibalism!). Also, you must provide more hiding places and more free space. Increase the size of the aquarium to at least 200 liters (53 gallons). If keeping a group, the animals must have enough space to not experience isolation. They become aggressive towards each other when stressed, which can cause severe damage to their aquarium companions. Axolotls are extraordinary and passionate creatures. However, you must provide the best conditions to enjoy their exotic beauty and unique behavior for at least 15 years.

Tank lid

Whether for aesthetic reasons or necessity, the aquarium cover is present in most aquariums. Some are made correctly, and others harm the proper gas exchange of the aquarium. It is widespread to see glass lids for sale in aquarium stores, and is aesthetically beautiful, but these do nothing good for the aquarium. Axolotls can jump out of an aquarium, so your aquarium needs a lid. Although it can be normal behavior, some reasons your pet may jump are related to stress. Some of these include:

- Large movement of people nearby;

- Your sudden appearance;

- Door knock noise;

- Too much noise or vibrations near the tank.

Some individuals do this based on instinct but many only do this when the water conditions are bad, such as:

- Too little oxygen;

- Temperature;

- Ammonia;

- Nitrate;

- Nitrite;

Although poorly documented, axolotls are said to practice jumping in their natural habitat; they do this to migrate to another environment, to look for food, or to maintain their species.

Screen covers are safe for jumping animals and provide excellent gas exchange between the water and the atmosphere. There are screen covers that are 1 cm in height (less than half an inch) that give the aquarium a beautiful look, and these are the best covers for large aquariums due to the great need for oxygenation. If you utilize this lid in your aquarium, focus on those with not too fine of a mesh, because the thinner the wire, the greater the chance of your axolotl being hurt if it jumps.

Not using any lid on the aquarium might seem like the best choice aesthetically, but many have lost their animals because they did not use any form of cover.

Substrate

The substrate is an integral part of any axolotl aquarium. This is the material that covers the bottom.

Axolotls require either a very thin or thick substrate, as this animal eats by sucking, so it can suck the food that falls to the bottom of the aquarium, thus sucking and swallowing substrate, which causes accidents and illnesses.

In addition, axolotls have a habit of biting the substrate out of curiosity, and in many cases end up swallowing it, which can be fatal. A safe granulometry (basically, the size of the grain) would be a substrate close in size to the head of an axolotl, but inevitably, this means there will be an accumulation of debris due to its large size.

Fine sand, similar in size to refined sugar, can be used; however, our amphibians will probably swallow it. But this will not have severe consequences, so it is an excellent option.

To sum up, the substrate for an axolotl must be one of these two options. Or else an incredibly thin substrate so if the animal swallows a little, it quickly leaves its body without causing problems like impaction. One final option is a substrate of high granulometry and heavy so the amphibian cannot suck it up and ingest it.

Filtration system

Being a 100 percent aquatic species, maintaining good water quality is the most crucial aspect of care you should observe for your axolotl. You must always closely supervise the quality of the renewal water that enters your aquariums; like all amphibians, these little animals can absorb all harmful substances that the water may contain through their skin.

Axolotls are sensitive to very high or even medium water flows. They prefer calm waters that are very well-oxygenated and clean. Practically all filters currently have flow control; in the case of systems without flow control, you must create some mechanism so that the current caused by the filtering system is "blocked," preventing current, or else you need to direct the linear flow of the pumps to the corner of the aquarium or even to the glass, so there will be oxygenation and filtration without so much current.

Another option is to place some decorations or plants in front of the filter that can serve as a shield to reduce the intensity of the flow. It's very important to provide optimal biological and mechanical filtration. Axolotls produce a considerable amount of debris and we must install the proper amount of media to provide optimal biological filtration for the corresponding number of animals.

As for your choice of filter, first, choose one recommended for the size of your aquarium and of good quality. For beginners, great options are Sponge, Hang-On, and Canister-type filters. They are efficient, easy to clean, and generally have water flow control.

Temperature control system

Probably one of the factors that most often kill axolotls in aquariums is the water temperature. These amphibians require cold water with an ideal range between 16° and 18° C (60.8-64.4°F). At temperatures above 23°C (73.4°F), they tend to feed more vigorously, but unfortunately, the axolotl may then suffer from acute stress and stop eating, and will die quickly.

The first symptoms of heat stress include food refusal, floating near the surface, and developing spots on their body; mucus loss is relatively common in these cases. Many enthusiasts maintain refrigerated areas with central air conditioners to prevent early loss of their axolotls. In my case, the chiller was an indispensable item in the maintenance of my pets. In some regions with milder climates, it is possible to use fans and coolers, especially in areas with subtropical temperatures; however, a cooler, in my experience, will always be one of the best maintenance options.

How to monitor the temperature of your aquarium
Aquarium temperature is often the first thing many aquarists test and try to control; it is a crucial factor in maintaining healthy axolotls. There are a few different ways to monitor the temperature in your aquarium. Many heaters and coolers have built-in temperature settings, but they can fail. Some are notoriously inaccurate; glass thermometers intended for aquariums are prone to breakage; cheap digital thermometers often fail after short periods and do not have built-in calibration.

For the most accurate temperature measurements, always use high-quality precision thermometers. With varying cable lengths and probe types, we can find a multitude of precise high thermometers for any professional or home aquarium.

Keeping an eye on the water temperature in our aquarium is essential, especially in regions where the temperature variation is significant.

Refrigeration in aquariums

When the aquarium heats up too much, the axolotl does not feel well, dissolved oxygen decreases, and serious problems arise. When it's cold, it's relatively easier to warm it up - just add a thermostat or a heater suitable for the size of the aquarium, and everything will be fine. But when the water is too hot, the situation is more complicated and can be more expensive than heating the aquarium. Three pieces of equipment are used for cooling aquariums: fans, chillers, and a Peltier cooler.

1. Fans

Fans use atmospheric air around the aquarium to evaporate the water. The fan itself does not cool the aquarium water in any way; the evaporation process, which depends on several factors, is what draws heat out of the water.

Evaporating water removes heat, reducing the system's temperature. However, several factors influence evaporation, such as relative air humidity, ambient temperature, salinity, the contact surface, and wind speed.

The combination of these factors means that the aquarium cooling depends directly on the amount of water that evaporates from the aquarium. Since the relative humidity of the air varies independent from human interference, evaporation and cooling capacity also differ. This is extremely bad for aquariums and is therefore a constant risk.

No matter how good they are, fans in excellent environmental conditions manage to cool an aquarium a maximum of 4°C (39°F) in relation to the external environment. This variation may be sufficient for mild external temperatures but not for scorching and humid summer days. A negative point of this cooling system is the water that evaporates from the aquarium. It is necessary to have a water replacement system in aquariums to avoid an increase of salinity.

Evaporation also has other implications, such as moistening the environment and encouraging rust. Although the salts in the aquarium water do not evaporate, tiny drops of water containing these salts are carried away by the force of the fans and can rust things in the environment.

2. Chiller
The chiller is the most established and reliable aquarium cooling system available. It does not depend on environmental conditions to function, but it tends to be costly because of its titanium alloy tubing. The chiller works the same way as a refrigerator, a compressor cools the refrigerant gas from the equipment, and this cools the titanium pipe through which the aquarium water passes. There's not much more to say about chillers, except they need to be correctly sized for the aquarium to be refrigerated. Though the chiller can be expensive, it lasts at least five years if properly used. Assembling a chiller is easy and works best when connected to a canister. The

water will go from the filter to the canister and back to your tank, so the hoses and connections for both must be of a compatible size.

Installation instructions:

- Connect the water inlet and outlet hoses to the top of your chiller;

- Turn on the pump so that the water starts to circulate through the chiller and returns to the aquarium;

- The chiller thermostat is usually already set. If not, adjust to the desired temperature;

- After being plugged in, the thermostat display will light up after a few seconds, and the chiller will start operating.

Of course, each brand will have its differences and correct handling instructions. It is essential to follow the manual for your device and, if in doubt, ask a specialist for help.

3. Peltier cooler

Peltier coolers work on the principle of the thermoelectric effect. This effect consists of passing an electric current between plates of conductors arranged deliberately, generating a cold and hot side. These coolers have been used with success, especially in small aquariums, due to the simplicity of construction, affordable price, and minimal space used. Still, there are more efficient options for aquariums with a greater volume of water.

This type of cooler needs an excellent heat dissipation system to function correctly. Cooling is a tricky issue in aquariums because of the high cost of having a chiller.

Aquarists sometimes understand the risk of using fans, but many have no idea just how risky it can be, so every year, some lose their salamander and give up on the hobby. On the other hand, taking a well-calculated risk can sometimes bring good results.

The decision of which equipment to use depends on the weather condition of the city you live in, where the aquarium is located, the aquarium's cooling needs, and the size of the aquarium.

Using hides

There are many reasons why you should add hiding places for your axolotls. Many don't feel safe unless they have somewhere they can hide. Lack of hiding places can often lead to animal stress, so giving your pet proper hiding places is a win-win situation. When the animals feel more comfortable, the aquarist ends up being rewarded with a range of their natural behaviors. Also, axolotls seem to love exploring aquarium objects.

What hiding places can you create?
You can get creative when decorating, making caves with the pipes or burying half of a flower pot in the aquarium and adding some large rocks inside, creating a more natural cave. Overall, you can do many things with DIY hidings and different types of material, so be creative!

1. Plants
Adding hardy or artificial plants to an aquarium will act as a unique refuge for your axolotl and be visually very appealing. Some plants and mosses are ideal, especially for hatchlings to hide. The dense growth of the plants

provides hiding places and mimics the natural environment of these salamanders. If live plants aren't your thing or don't adapt well to the aquarium environment, consider adding artificial ones.

2. Rocks

For those who like a more natural aquarium, adding some rocks to form hiding places is a great idea. When well-placed, they can create biological cave-like structures that shelter most aquatic animals. Just remember to plan ahead what you will do in the aquarium and make sure they are very well-placed to avoid accidents.

3. Aquarium ornaments

Decorations are also a great addition to the aquarium when you want to create hiding places, as they provide slits where the axolotl can hide. When adding decorations, be aware that there are no corners or sharp edges that could cause accidents. Also, make sure the decorations are made specifically for aquariums.

4. Driftwood and roots

Adding logs and roots is a good idea; this natural landscaping provides suitable shelter, such as caves and crevices. In addition, adding these hiding place for your pet will further encourage their natural behavior. But again, watch out for edges and corners.

5. Clay pots or PVC pipes

We don't always have the money to buy ornaments and decorations for an aquarium. So, adding small clay pots and some PVC pipes can be a good alternative and often cheaper than many other types of decoration. In addition to functioning as a place where axolotls can hide, these ornaments can also serve as a spawning space for animals.

Water

Aquarium water is the most critical component for your axolotls. Unfortunately, water quality is often over-looked. The best aquarium water should be as pure and clean as possible, free from toxic substances such as chlorine, heavy metals, and nitrogen compounds. While humans can flee a smoke-filled room, for exam-ple, axolotls cannot escape if their water becomes toxic or dangerous. These salamanders inhabit cold, alkaline, and mineralized waters.

It is necessary to understand the chemistry of water to guarantee the right properties for your animals. If these parameters are observed, and the tank's filtration system ensures that the water is biologically healthy, we have achieved "quality water." This is accomplished by test-ing the water. Generally speaking, aquarium testing is divided into primary and secondary. However, all tests are essential.

But to maintain the water parameters, primary tests are considered indispensable. After all, this is how you will check factors such as temperature, toxicity, and pH, among others. These are fundamental conditions for the maintenance of life in an aquarium. The chemical and physical properties of water that must be taken into account for this purpose and measured regularly are pH, KH (carbonate hardness), GH (total hardness), tempera-ture, levels of nitrogen compounds (ammonia, nitrite, and nitrate), and oxygen.

pH

When we talk about the pH of the water, we are referring to the fact that it can be either acidic, neutral, or primary, which is the same as being alkaline. pH stands for "potential of hydrogen," a chemical indicator that evaluates the concentration of hydrogen ions in a substance as an aqueous solution.

The pH values are shown on a numerical scale that goes from 0 to 14 and which is used to specify the acidity or basicity of a solution, with the value seven corresponding to "neutral"; values below 7 to 0 already correspond to "acidic" and values above 7 to 14 are equivalent to "basic," or "alkaline." Axolotls survive without problems at a slightly acidic pH, around 6.8; however, it is best to keep them in water with a more alkaline pH, about 7.5.

Therefore, any adjustments that have consequences for the pH should never be carried out suddenly but only in several progressive steps to minimize the shock this can cause. While this subject may be better suited to a discussion in a book dealing with freshwater aquarium chemistry, hobbyists need to develop a solid understanding of why so-called general hardness and carbonate hardness (abbreviated GH and KH, respectively) are not the same, as this is a common misconception among hobbyists. The misunderstanding may be because there are many explanations about the differences between these parameters in the literature.

Testing the pH

One of the most frequently tested and essential parameters in aquariums is pH. No matter what type of aquarium you have, knowing the optimal pH range and monitoring it is crucial to success.

Water chemistry is necessary to successfully maintain an aquarium, but not all tanks require the same chemistry. pH plays a significant role in this difference. As the pH of the water increases, so does the percentage of ammonia in its most toxic form. Ammonia excretion is also impaired at higher pH levels, limiting an organism's ability to eliminate waste.

Keeping your aquarium pH stable and in the optimal ranges reduces stress on your aquatic animals, helping them to resist disease and tolerate other stressors. Maintaining an optimal pH can also dramatically improve the axolotl's growth, behavior, and overall appearance. With aquariums' processes and environmental factors, it is normal for the pH to vary over time. That's why you must carry out tests periodically.

Traditionally, pH is measured in aquariums with test strips (e.g., litmus paper) or color comparison chemical test kits. These methods are inaccurate, though, especially within the limited range of aquariums. Litmus paper can become contaminated, which leads to incorrect results, while test kits are subjective, as they rely on the human eye to detect a color match. It is best to use a pH electrode and a meter for optimal results and more accessible measurements. While this may seem like a lot for a beginner, companies produce a wide range of affordable, accurate, and easy-to-use pH meters that are great for aquarists with varying budgets.

GH

GH is an abbreviation for "General Hardness." It is the sum of divalent cations (ions with a charge of $+^2$) in solution, including elements such as calcium, magnesium, strontium, and many heavier metals such as iron and copper.

As magnesium and calcium ions are much more abundant in water than other divalent cations, GH is essentially the combined concentration of magnesium and calcium ions. Therefore, it does not cover concentrations of monovalent cations or anions (with a charge of $+/-^1$), such as sodium and chloride.

Testing the GH

Some GH test kits can distinguish calcium concentration from other divalent cations in a sample. This makes it possible to obtain a rough estimate of the magnesium concentration in the solution (subtracting the calcium concentration from the measured GH leaves the magnesium concentration).

KH

KH, or "carbonate hardness," measures the amount of carbonates and bicarbonates in water, which affects the buffering capacity of the water.

To understand buffering capacity, think of it as a sponge. When we add acid, the "sponge" absorbs it, and if the sponge is large, it will absorb even more, but if it is small, it will fill up and lose its capacity to absorb more. That is, KH higher (larger sponge) and KH lower (small sponge). Because of these differences, low KH absorbs little acid, and the water quickly acidifies.

KH is a measure of the alkalinity of the solution. Alkalinity measures the concentration of the anionic solution of carbonate, hydroxide, phosphate, silicate, and borate. Carbonate hardness is said to be "temporary" hardness because the released carbonates react quickly with the acids in the sample. Once this happens, the alkalinity is depleted. Permanent hardness is the concentration of ions that cannot be removed by boiling water, usually nitrates, chlorides, sulfates, etc. Temporary hardness is the concentration of ions quickly released by boiling water.

We can generally say that a solution with high GH will have high TDS (total dissolved solids), but a solution with high TDS will not necessarily have high GH (TDS takes all ions into account, such as sodium and chloride, and GH does not). Understanding these details in depth will help you better control the water parameters in your aquarium.

Ammonia, nitrite, and nitrate
For inhabitants to live in a healthy environment in your aquarium, it is crucial to maintain the water quality. Aquariums with poor maintenance will produce toxic substances in the water, which can lead to the death of fish and other living beings. One of these poisonous substances is ammonia. It forms through the decomposition of organic matter, such as feces, urine, food scraps, dead leaves, etc. In nature, whether in a lake, river, or sea (where the volume of water is obviously much greater than in an aquarium), because the amount of water is so large, the ammonia produced by the fish is quickly diluted and disappears. But an aquarium has much less water to dilute the ammonia, so will have higher ammonia concentrations.

Ammonia is a highly toxic substance, and a small amount can quickly burn an axolotl's gills. It can even kill or at least cause severe and permanent damage in higher concentrations. The nitrogen cycle is the biological process where bacteria will convert ammonia (NH_3) to nitrite (NO_2), and then the nitrite is converted to nitrate (NO_3).

Ammonia > Nitrite > Nitrate

To simplify it a bit, the nitrogen cycle in the aquarium is a process of forming a colony of beneficial bacteria that will be responsible for controlling/reducing the toxic substances in the water that are lethal to the aquarium's inhabitants. This process is essential for anyone setting up a new aquarium. In the aquarium hobby, a term often used for this process is "cycling the aquarium."

Excreta and other decaying organic matter produce ammonia, which is highly toxic to fish. However, the oxygen-dependent bacteria, called Nitrosomonas, oxidize ammonia/ammonia to nitrites, which are slightly less harmful. Nitrite is toxic to fish but not as harmful as ammonia. Bacteria of the genus Nitrobacter or Nitrobacterium then convert the nitrite into nitrate.

Nitrate, a by-product of the nitrogen cycle, is generally considered harmless to axolotls at low levels. Algae and plants then consume the nitrate, naturally lowering its concentration level.

Testing the ammonia and nitrite

These tests indicate the presence of nitrogen in the water. This substance is formed from the process of decomposition of organic matter. If the aquarium test indicates high concentration, you should perform a partial aquarium water change. In addition, so that nitrogen levels do not rise again, you must improve the biological phase of the filtering system and maintenance carried out in shorter intervals.

The cycling process

We should bring our axolotl home after the aquarium is adequately set up, with the water and feeding parameters already arranged. Most importantly, the aquarium water must be mature enough to receive its first inhabitants. By "mature" I mean that it has already gone through the cycling period.

The nitrogen cycle

All material of organic origin generated by decomposition, whether from food scraps or the waste of the inhabitants of an aquarium, invariably ends up turning into ammonia. Ammonia is a very harmful substance for fish and needs to be removed somehow. The accumulation of this substance in the aquarium leads to death for most fish by poisoning or asphyxiation.

In nature, there are aerobic bacteria (meaning they can survive and grow in an oxygenated environment) called Nitrosomonas that transform ammonia into nitrous acid (or *nitrites*). These bacteria use the energy generated by the reaction in their metabolism. Unfortunately, the nitrites generated are also quite harmful to fish.

Fortunately, another group of aerobic bacteria called Nitrobacter oxidizes nitrites into *nitrates*, which are less toxic than nitrites. These bacteria also feed on the energy released by the transformation. The nitrates formed are less harmful than either ammonia or nitrites but must also be removed, though nitrates are a source of nutrients for plants, so it's important to have some in a closed system like an aquarium.

The time required for such colonies to establish themselves in aquariums varies with factors like temperature, type of substrate, pH, and oxygen content of the water, making it difficult to pinpoint the exact time but, as a rule, it takes 30 to 40 days. It takes about 8 to 10 days for the bacteria that consume ammonia to establish themselves and start acting.

When this happens, nitrite levels rise, reaching their maximum by the 15th day. This is when the other colony of bacteria begins turning the nitrites into nitrates. Note that, under normal conditions, nitrates rise indefinitely, exceeding the concentration of nitrites at around 20 to 25 days. By then, ammonia should be under control. And when the nitrites are finally at zero, this is a sign that there are already enough bacteria in the aquarium to consume these substances. But remember that the concentration of nitrates will be very high at this time.

This is when we need to do a partial water change, to reduce these levels and make the water ready to receive its first inhabitants. Note that the times quoted in this book are only approximate, because times can vary dramatically depending on several factors.

Cycling step by step
The nitrifying bacteria will be present in the aquarium within a few days. For cycling to happen, they need to

be fixed somewhere. They will be present throughout the aquarium, but their incredible efficiency will occur where they settle and the oxygen flow is available.

The substrate at the bottom of the aquarium is an excellent place for bacteria to fix themselves, but you must sufficiently aerate it. For this reason, it is common to use fixation media inside the filters for such bacteria, as the constant flow of water guarantees the oxygen necessary for the reactions.

Aquarists use the media in their filters most: sponges, bio-balls, and ceramic rings. The larger the surface of attachment for the bacteria, the larger their colonies will be, guaranteeing the ready consumption of these pollutants.

Now let's go through the steps to setting up your aquarium:

1. Assemble the aquarium, add the substrate and decoration;
2. Add the water;
3. Turn on your filtration system.

Take advantage of the days of waiting for the cycling process to read as much as you can about the hobby and about axolotls, so you can become more and more familiar with this fascinating hobby! Also use the opportunity to place your plants, so they have time to set their roots in the substrate. Give them the amount of light they need daily. Try to keep the temperature as close to the ideal temperature as possible so the bacteria will multiply as quickly as possible.

Some aquarists use some source of ammonia to "start" the formation of bacteria colonies, but this is not necessary. Remember that water is a way of life for thousands of microorganisms that will come to exist in your aquarium, and their metabolisms will already be a source of ammonia.

Dead plant tissue is also a source of ammonia. Therefore, though many do, there is no need to add pieces of meat or fish. Note that very high concentrations of ammonia inhibit bacteria growth.

The aquarist should monitor the cycling process of the aquarium by periodically measuring the concentrations of both ammonia and nitrite.

When both are zeroed, it's time to do a partial water change (30 to 40 percent) to reduce nitrates, and the aquarium will be ready to receive its first inhabitants. Watch out! Don't put all the fish in at once. Give your bacteria time to get used to the new load of waste before adding your new salamander.

At first, even after cycling is complete, the aquarium water still needs to be 100 percent matured. This takes at least six months. Therefore, ammonia and nitrite tests must continue to be done, at least once a week, to monitor these levels and ensure that the environment is suitable for your axolotls.

Oxygenation in aquariums
Of all the gases in the atmosphere, we and all other animals and plants primarily use oxygen to produce energy to stay alive. In aquariums, oxygen plays a fundamental role in several processes, from the growth of plants and animals to nitrifying bacteria, the oxidation of toxic chemical compounds, the control of pathogenic organisms, and several other processes.

The oxygenation of the aquarium occurs through the gas exchange between the aquarium and atmospheric water. One factor influencing the amount of dissolved oxygen in the water is the temperature; the higher the temperature, the lower the oxygen concentration. In an aquarium with no water circulation, the O^2 saturation point happens (if it ever happens) only on the water's surface.

Thus, in these cases, oxygen distribution is not uniform, which is why good circulation is necessary. The water becomes rich in oxygen near the surface, and the concentration decreases with depth. This information is essential when we primarily think about filtering. An essential factor you can change to improve the exchange of gases between water and the atmosphere is decreasing the surface tension in the water. Surface tension is that film that forms on the surface of the water. For example, the surface tension that is prevalent in lakes allows insects to float on the water.

Air pumps minimally change the amount of dissolved oxygen in the water because of the pressure of the water column on the air bubble. The most significant effect of air pumps on oxygenation is when they rock the surface a little and reduce the surface tension. The best way to reduce surface tension is to cause turbulence on the water's surface. The greater the area of turbulence and the amount of water involved in the movement, the better the gas exchange. It will hardly reach saturation, but it will be enough to maintain all life forms in the aquarium.

Now that we have seen how vital oxygen is, it should be mentioned that in an aquarium, it is a limiting factor in several processes, such as the growth of aquarium inhabitants, bacteria, conversion of ammonia and nitrite to less toxic compound levels, and plant growth.

Chlorine and chloramine

Companies that supply water in your area most likely use chlorine or chloramine to treat the water and limit the growth of bacteria and other dangerous contaminants. For most people, this makes no difference, but for an aquarium owner, it can be the fine line between life and death for their animals.

Chlorine is a gas dissolved in tap water that helps kill microorganisms that may inadvertently enter a city's water supply pipe. However, the chlorine concentration needed to treat public water sources successfully is high enough to be lethal to your axolotls.

Chloramine is a combination of chlorine and ammonia. Ammonia joins the gas to keep it in solution longer, but unlike pure chlorine, which dissipates quickly when exposed to air, chloramine stays in the water for a long time. This is very good for companies providing safe drinking water from contaminants like bacteria. However, it is not very good for those who like to raise fish at home and want to use tap water to fill their aquarium.

First, an old trick of letting water sit in open buckets or aquariums with air pumps on doesn't work like it used to. You can let the water sit for a few days, but the chloramine will remain. Second, you must ensure the water is free of chlorine and ammonia. It is important to know that homemade conditioners remove chlorine but not chloramine.

The good news is that these elements are easily removed from the water through aquarium water conditioners. The easiest way to find out what's in tap water is to call your city's water supply company and ask what they use to treat it. However, not all water conditioners neutralize chloramine, so choose the best products on the market.

Also, you can always test your water. Buy an ammonia test kit and use it in your tap water. If there is any ammonia in the test, it is almost certain that chloramine is present. Using a good water conditioner to eliminate chlorine and chloramine from your tap water is the best way to ensure the safety of your axolotl.

Types of water to use

Next, we will analyze the most frequently used waters so you can determine which is the best to put in your axolotl aquarium.

Rainwater
Today, given the pollution in our air, it would be a terrible mistake to use rainwater in an aquarium because when the rain falls, it promotes a kind of purification in the atmosphere of the pollution residue caused by factories, cars, etc. In addition, this type of water does not contain many minerals; it would have to undergo a chemical treatment before you could safely use it for your axolotl.

Bottled water
The composition of commercial water varies from brand to brand, as it is already ready, so the exact composition of this water depends on its origin. There are, in most brands, traits in common, such as pH or very high or very low compounds such as magnesium nitrate, potassium nitrate, sodium nitrate, calcium sulfate, and sodium

chloride. This information is all provided on the packaging itself. Note that this water is not cheap and if you have, for example, a 200-liter (53 gallon) aquarium, filling it and doing partial changes could be costly, but it is a decent option for good water.

Tap water

Tap water is, in fact, the water most used by aquarists. It is easy to obtain, and its negligible cost makes it very comfortable to use, but it must first undergo treatment to become suitable for aquarium. You should use a good water conditioner to bind heavy metal ions, chlorine, chloramine, and other toxicants harmful to axolotls. The idea is to conduct all the tests on this water to know if there is any harmful substance or if it needs some adjustment of pH, KH, etc.

Deionized water or RO

This would be the best water for aquariums, as it is the only one that guarantees a substance that is truly free of any harmful element. This type of water is obtained through special filtration using resins or membranes. When water passes through it, it tends to be a little acidic, but this is an easy problem to solve with products that can be used as alkalizer.

Never use this water directly in your axolotl aquarium. All types of pure water must undergo chemical treatment to adjust hardness, pH, and other factors.

The best water for your aquarium

No water is perfect for use in an aquarium. However, some types will best adapt to your needs, time, and resources. Whatever you choose, you need to pay close attention to chlorine, and minimize it. Before filling your aquarium, ensure your water is ideal for consumption.

Lighting system

Axolotls do not need special lighting, since these animals prefer to live in dark places. The idea is to use excellent quality luminaires because they do not heat up too much. However, you must remember that these amphibians do not have eyelids, so light can hurt their eyes.

Light is vital for salamanders to know when it is day and night, but this is easily achieved through indirect light reaching the aquarium. Good quality LEDs can be suitable, especially those with brightness control and those in which you can change the focus of the light to reduce the direct incidence of solid light on the bottom of the tank.

The main factor in lighting has to do with keeping plants alive. Good quality lighting depends on the plants you want to keep in the aquarium. If you opt to keep heavily planted or high-tech plants, you must keep several hiding places and shaded places for your axolotl. Floating plants are great for this. If you want to keep plants and still have typical low lighting, consider plants known as low-tech, such as Anubias, Amazon sword, and Java fern.

Artificial vs. live plants

Usually, freshwater aquariums contain artificial or natural plants because, in addition to making axolotls feel closer to their habitat, they offer them a place to hide and feel safe. However, there are differences between artificial and natural plants. And now you're probably wondering which options are more viable. Both artificial aquarium plants and natural plants have positive and negative points. Thus, you must consider the pros and cons before deciding on the best option.

Natural plants can offer an environment closer to your salamander's habitat, although they require greater care. They can be more work in aquarium maintenance, requiring frequent pruning since they can grow without adequate control. In addition, many also require adequate lighting, a fertile substrate that provides the nutrients they need, liquid supplementation, and even the injection of CO_2 directly into the aquarium. Finally, you must avoid certain types of fertilizers, as they can be toxic to your axolotl.

When opting for natural plants, you may also find it more difficult to decorate or organize the aquarium, as the roots of the plants can make the process complicated. Also, axolotls love to bite plants and pull them out of their planting site!

Aquariums with artificial plants can be almost as beautiful as natural ones. Despite being mostly made of plastic, some can look almost real. These plants may even seem more practical because they are easy to remove for cleaning, can be replaced if the aquarist so desires, and are much more durable than natural plants. However, although artificial aquarium plants are much easier to deal with, they also have some disadvantages. Some may look real, but for the most part, they don't look as beautiful as natural plants and, in some cases, have colors that don't even exist in nature.

In addition, even though they are designed to stick to the gravel, due to their plastic bottom, they can float to the top of the aquarium. Great artificial aquarium plants are heavy enough to stay where they are placed and look very real. But, depending on the size, these can be much more expensive. And finally, an essential factor to be considered is that, because they are artificial, there is a significant risk that the material they are made from is harmful to your amphibian's health, so it's crucial to make sure they are specific to your purpose and safe. In any case, just like natural plants, artificial plants provide the feeling of shelter and a realistic environment closer to the amphibian habitat.

So both types of plants have advantages and disadvantages, and your choice will depend on your feelings, perspective and needs.

Plants for your aquarium

If you choose to put live plants in your axolotl's aquarium, remember to choose plants that don't need a lot of light or large-grained substrates, which the axolotl can swallow. There are several species of plants that require little or no care. These are referred to as low-tech, or undemanding.

These are easily obtained and do not require a lot of technology to be maintained, hence the name. These plants do very well in a substrate like sand without fertilization (which can be toxic to amphibians) or additional light supplementation (since axolotls do not have eyelids and prefer to live in low-light environments). Unlike the planted (high-tech) aquarium, where the investment is higher in technological devices and requires more regular care by the aquarist, low-maintenance or low-tech plants offer the same beauty.

1. Echinodorus amazonicus

Echinodorus amazonicus can be grown in a substrate with few nutrients and will have a very healthy development. It will be a little smaller under these conditions, but it will still be a large plant. In a fertile and nutrient-rich substrate, it tends to grow too big, throwing leaves out of the water and making life a little complicated to maintain.

2. Anubias barteri' Coffeefolia'

Anubias barteri 'Coffeefolia' has this name because of its beautiful leaves that are reminiscent of the coffee shrub. When young, the leaves have an exuberant copper color and turn dark green as they age. As it is a plant that does not like much light, place it in shady areas. It doesn't need CO_2, but its addition helps in development.

3. Bacopa caroliniana

Bacopa caroliniana is a beautiful plant ideal for beginner aquarists. This is because it is an easy-to-maintain plant that adapts to almost any environment. Providing light, CO_2, and partial water changes, you will have a wonderful and pleasant plant in your aquarium. Its propagation is done by cutting and replanting the branch.

4. Microsorum sp.

Known as Java fern, this is one of the easiest aquatic plants to keep and, as such, is a crucial starting point for the beginning aquarist. This ease of maintenance, combined with its ability to root in rocks, logs, and other surfaces that are usually unavailable for planting, has ensured the longevity of this species in the aquascaping hobby.

Medium-light is sufficient for optimal growth, although higher and lower light values are well tolerated. Like

Anubias plants, *Microsorum* has a rhizome from which both leaves and roots develop. Therefore, it can be tied to a rock, for example, with thread or other materials. After a few months, the roots will set, and you can remove the binding.

If you want to plant this in the substrate, you must be careful to bury only the roots and not the rhizome. While exceptional fertilization and CO_2 supplementation are unnecessary, maintaining good water circulation and oxygenation is essential for good growth.

5. Java moss

This species is easy to grow, tolerating and growing in a wide range of water conditions after acclimatization. This plant is undemanding as far as lighting. However, it will grow dense and lush at high light levels. In low light, the plant will be darker and slimmer. While CO_2 and fertilizing will increase growth rates, this moss will also thrive without them.

To attach it to logs, spread it over the desired location and wrap it with a fishing line or cotton thread until the moss is well protected. Then it will grow and adhere to the object, forming a dark green cushion. Its branching is irregular, with long leaves of approximately two milli-meters along the stems. If not pruned regularly, it will quickly form a soft tangle.

It is easily pruned and propagated by simply cutting off excess growth with suitable scissors. You can then relo-cate this excess growth to a new surface.

How to make a Java moss wall

Many of these mosses can be used in the aquarium. There are several ways to fix them and have a great result;

one way is to plant mosses on stainless steel screens. Be creative, and with this technique, you can fill small spaces, use them as a "moss wall," low-tech low maintenance carpet, or just as a refuge for your axolotl.

Required items:

- Scissors with fine tips;
- Clamp;
- Stainless steel screen;
- Portion of moss;
- Fine nylon fishing or sewing thread.

How to make:

- Cut the canvas to the desired size;
- Chop the moss and spread it over the entire surface of the screen, filling all the spaces;
- Leave the moss uniform and apply light pressure to fix it well on the canvas;
- Tie the moss with nylon thread or even ordinary sewing thread;
- Cut the leftovers from the thread.

That's it. Now you can fix your wall wherever you want.

Introducing your axolotl

Now that your aquarium is decorated and cycled, it's time for the most exciting part: bringing home your new axolotl!

Adaptation process

To adapt your new aquatic friend to his new home, I have some essential tips for you to reduce stress and future problems in your salamander. The ideal is that before entering the aquarium, your axolotl undergoes a slight adaptation; it is a straightforward procedure and just requires a little time. In this adaptation, you will equalize the water parameters of the bag that comes with the axolotl. This process is called acclimatization.

For your salamander to adapt successfully, it is essential to acclimate the new inhabitant to the parameters of the aquarium. During the journey home, the pH and temperature of their bag will change. On scorching days, the temperature can go up, and when it's colder, it can go down.

By staying inside the bag for some time, aquatic animals generate a large amount of ammonia and this, consequently, causes the pH to drop and become very acidic, harming their health. Not making the correct adaptation will most likely cause unnecessary stress and even heat or pH shock, leading to your new axolotl's death.

Keep your newly acquired pet somewhere dark on your way home from the store. The pet store will likely place your pet in a clear plastic bag inflated with oxygen. Keeping the axolotl in the dark will make things easier for it during the trip. Of course, you must head straight to your house; the shorter the time, the better.

When you get home, leave the bag floating in the aquarium for 10 to 15 minutes to equalize the temperatures. Measure the temperature with a thermometer. It is ideal for letting the bag float longer. Once this is done, your next step is to add amounts of aquarium water into the bag every five minutes to equalize the pH. It is also imperative to have a pH test to compare the parameters of the aquarium with those of the bag.

When temperature and pH are the same, you can introduce your axolotl to the aquarium. However, the bag water needs to be discarded and should not be mixed with the aquarium water; this is necessary because of the low quality of the water in the bag, and because it contains pathogens. Finally, since some of the aquarium water was used to acclimate the axolotl, you must replace it, but be sure to treat it with water conditioner before pouring it into the aquarium.

Many novice axolotl owners don't realize that during their capture, when placed in the bag, the axolotl becomes stressed and loses mucus, which protects it against bacteria. This is why it's common for the animal to leave the store healthy and the next day to present fungi and parasites in its new home. This happens because it has entered a new vulnerable environment with low immunity. However, these parasites or fungi were already present in its body. Therefore, this acclimatization process is fundamental.

Finally, it is normal for the amphibian to exhibit a dull color at first, as well as accelerated breathing, and to remain stationary at the bottom of the aquarium. Don't worry - these are signs of transportation stress and being in an unfamiliar environment. Soon your pet will become used to its new environment, exhibiting its normal behavior, and its coloring will return.

More than one axolotl

If you already have an axolotl and want to add another to the same aquarium, or if you decided to buy two at once, there are some basic rules to follow. But stay calm; keeping multiple axolotls together is certainly possible. But it's important to note that for this to work, the animals must be the same size; otherwise, cannibalism and bites can occur.

Another extremely important factor is that the aquarium has enough space, including hiding places, for all the animals. Therefore, you must add a minimum of 40 liters (10.5 gallons) for each additional animal.

Keep in mind, though, that axolotls are solitary animals, so they won't feel depressed if they spend their entire life alone in the aquarium.

Introducing an axolotl to an aquarium with other animals

If you already have an axolotl and want to add a companion, you must first quarantine your new animal. Quarantine is a period of isolation somewhere other than the main aquarium, where new animals spend time before being introduced into the main aquarium. In most cases, two or three weeks is a sufficient amount of time, and 40 days is usually the maximum.

Isolation of the first fish destined for a new aquarium is optional, although useful. Quarantine has a dual purpose: to reduce the risk of infection by the pathological agents that may be carried by the new axolotls, and to allow the amphibian to recover from the physical stress accumulated during transport. This entire process must be carried out in a different aquarium, known as a 'quarantine. or hospital aquarium.'

This aquarium doesn't need to be very big - at most 60 liters (16 gallons) - to hold the salamander for a short time. Put a small filter in it; with media already cycled, you should do a total water change daily. The water quality in this aquarium must always be perfect. This aquarium does not need substrate or hardscape, but must be in a quieter area of your home, where the axolotl is not constantly disturbed by people, and it must also have adequate temperature, hardness, and pH conditions.

Acclimatize and place your axolotl inside, then keep an eye out for the next few days, paying attention to your pet's behavior and body. Although the axolotl may appear healthy, it could have an underlying disease that will present itself during the observation period. If they show signs of illness, parasite, or fungus, you should immediately take it to a veterinarian and start treatment.

During quarantine, axolotls should be watched daily. Try to make sure the routine and type of food, temperature, pH, etc., are all similar to the main aquarium so they will get used to it. This period is also beneficial to strengthen the pet, since it often arrives weak from the store. Even if nothing unusual happens in the beginning, keep it in quarantine for at least the minimum period, as cycles of parasites take several weeks, so can take a while to manifest.

If you follow this process, you will have few, if any, problems with animals that are new to the main aquarium. The risk of illness and outbreaks is also much lower. Remember, the quarantine aquarium is not a luxury item. It is a basic aquarium, which should be considered an integral piece of equipment and should include a filter or heater. Without quarantine, we risk spreading diseases and other illnesses to the entire aquarium population.

Tank mates (or not) for axolotls

Although axolotls can live with other animals, including its own species, I strongly recommend keeping your animal alone, or at most with other axolotls of the same size and temperament. But, if you still want fish or invertebrates in your tank, some species may be suitable. Just don't expect the perfection and harmony you often find in a standard community aquarium.

The most important thing is to look for peaceful species that will not nibble the axolotl and those that need the same water parameters to live. You can keep some species of shrimp (like ghost and cherry) without problems and with a low risk of accidents. If you keep these invertebrates with your axolotl, introduce a large, healthy population to the aquarium, as the salamander is sure to eat some of these delicious snacks.

Still, on invertebrates, some hobbyists defend the use of snails in these aquariums, which is a somewhat controversial topic. Snails are animals that degrade water quality and consume a large part of the aquarium's alkaline reserve, quickly acidifying the water. In addition, axolotls will try to eat them, which can cause intestinal impaction, similar to when these animals gnaw on gravel from the substrate. If you still want to include these mollusks, choose the smallest species you can find.

In the case of fish, the accident factor is more significant; fish are curious animals that will hardly resist taking a nip of the feathery gills of your axolotl. Therefore, you should choose small, peaceful species. On the other hand, these animals will be constantly chased, bitten, and eaten by axolotls, who see them as a snack. Endlers are perfect for this purpose, but smaller guppies and livebearers can also be used.

In the end, though it is possible to keep axolotls with companions, I strongly recommend keeping them alone.

Maintaining your tank

The most important part of owning any aquatic animal is maintaining the water quality and general health of the tank. There are many questions about the best way to clean your aquarium. After how long should it undergo maintenance? What are suitable products? What steps are included in efficient cleaning?

These are common questions, along with many others, asked by those considering having an axolotl as a pet. It is also crucial information because if cleaning and maintenance of the aquarium are not carried out properly, the animals will almost surely become sick and can even die.

Aquarium maintenance means constantly being attentive, continuously checking the quality of the water through tests, and always observing the behavior of the axolotls and the conditions in which they are found, such as water temperature, turbidity (cloudiness or haziness of the water), and luminosity (brightness).

As much as the regularity of maintenance changes due to characteristics like filtration efficiency, number of animals, aquarium volume, etc., at least once a week a partial renewal of the aquarium water should be done.

The more water you remove, the better, but most aquarists remove 30 to 60 percent of the water volume; this is carried out with the aid of a siphon, hose, and bucket. This is also the time to clean the decorations, glass, and filtering system. This will require all electrical components to be turned off and cleaned as well.

How to perform the correct maintenance

Please note: Disassembling the aquarium and washing everything directly under a faucet is not necessary, or even ideal. While the concentration of toxicants drops to zero, all the biology that had developed in the aquarium is also destroyed, making it very difficult for the animals to survive and requiring you to cycle the tank again.

The basic function of maintenance and water changes is to remove impurities and nitrogen, dirt accumulated on the bottom, and restore the alkalinity of the water. Of course, each aquarium's requirements for water changes vary, so what we discuss here is simply a general guide. On average, the frequency of water changes should be weekly, or at most once every 15 days, with shifts starting at 30 percent of the aquarium's total volume. Eventually, if water conditions worsen, you can make a more significant (even complete) change, or increase the frequency of changes. Water changes should be done using a siphon.

Material required:

- Siphon;

- Clean bucket, exclusively for the aquarium (you will use this bucket to draw water and then treat and replenish the new water);

- Soft sponge or glass cleaners;

- Great quality water conditioner.

The first step is to turn off the pumps and heaters; you can start by cleaning the inside of the windows using a sponge or cleaners. It is important to emphasize that you should never use any product or untreated water in aquarium maintenance.

The next step is to use the siphon, which works using gravity: the aquarium is higher than the bucket, and after "starting" the siphon, you drain the water from the aquarium into the bucket. You can fill the siphon at the tap or suck water from the aquarium directly through the siphon.

The end of the siphon inside the aquarium is wider than the tube, so there is not enough pressure to suck the gravel, and only the dirt is removed; you might even lightly stir the substrate with the siphon, taking the opportunity to clean the bottom and remove food remains and fish waste. Removing decorations and objects is essential to expose debris or dirt trapped in them. Siphon the aquarium removing any dirt you see. After removing the desired amount of water, stop the process.

It is worth mentioning that you should never remove animals from the aquarium, but be sure to carry out maintenance calmly and methodically. It is essential to treat the water you will place in the aquarium to remove chlorine and other products, in addition to making it similar to the aquarium water in terms of pH, hardness, and temperature; for this, use the conditioner product and the bucket.

As for cleaning external or internal filters that use filter material, the more you clean, the longer the filter materials last, and the better the water quality, so I recommend cleaning the materials that retain dirt once a week and changing the filters. Elements wear out (such as activated carbon) every 30-40 days. The pump's impellers and filtering media must also be cleaned periodically, and done according to the manufacturer's instructions.

Decorations should be washed under the tap and cleaned with the help of a sponge or brush so you can remove algae.

Dealing with your axolotl poop

Axolotls are known to be dirty animals; they quickly degrade water quality, generating a large amount of waste. Much of this waste comes from the axolotl's breath, epithelial (outer layer of their body's surface) mucus, and, most importantly, its poop.

This is why maintenance of good water quality means the removal of the feces of these animals. Their stool is easy to recognize; it looks like a milky and gelatinous bag filled with dark or even reddish pieces - this color depends on the food they are ingesting.

It breaks down quickly, spreading and soiling the entire aquarium, so removing it with a net is not always the best option. Instead, the idea is to actively remove the feces through suction. You can do this with the help of a siphon, a large pipette, or even a turkey baster. The amount and frequency that these salamanders defecate depends on the type of food and how often they feed. Generally speaking, baby axolotls produce poop once a day, while juveniles and adults produce droppings less frequently. They usually defecate a few hours after eating.

It is possible that, with the movement of the axolotls, their poop breaks up and mixes with the substrate. They might also eat their waste, though this is nothing to worry about, as it does not cause problems. Keeping an eye on your salamander's poop, as strange as it may seem, is vital to maintaining good water quality and knowing if your animal has any problems, such as impaction.

Lack of defecation also occurs when animals are overfed. If you notice that your axolotl is not pooping, do not feed it again until it has defecated. If the problem persists, enlist the help of a veterinarian, and also do so if the stools are whitish or any other unusual color.

The ideal is to remove the poop right after they defecate, but obviously this is not always possible, so weekly maintenance is sufficient.

Ten common mistakes people make with axolotls

1. Use uncycled tanks

This is undoubtedly the main mistake among inexperienced aquarists. Aquariums that are not yet adequately cycled will not have enough bacteria to carry out the nitrogen cycle. Water degradation will occur quickly, followed by the death of your axolotl from intoxication. Always properly cycle your aquariums before introducing any animals.

2. Use gravel as substrate

This is another prevalent mistake, especially in impulsive purchases. Axolotls feed by suction, so they can suck up stones from the substrate and end up with internal problems, leading to their death. Always use fine sand or a bare bottom.

3. Use filters with a strong flow

Filters with a strong flow, in addition to pulling at the axolotls and causing accidents, will stress them and make them expend incredible energy because they will have to be constantly moving. Always use filters with flow regulation.

4. Not having cooling equipment

Axolotls inhabit calmer waters, but it is common for the unsuspecting and ill-informed hobbyist to think it is a tropical water animal and turn on a heater to warm the water, which will lead to problems. Always have a cooling system to keep the temperature stable and your axolotl healthy.

5. Use fertilizers or medicines

These salamanders are bare-skinned, absorbing and potentially suffering from whatever is in the water. Never use plant fertilizers, drugs, or elements like iodine without the recommendation of a veterinarian.

6. Handle the axolotl and remove it from the water

Never touch your axolotl! This strips away its protective mucus layer, leaving it exposed to bacteria and contamination. And, like any aquatic animal, you should never take it out of the water. This will cause the animal to suffer from suffocation and stress.

7. Put it together with fish

As discussed in the topic regarding tank mates, it is best to keep your axolotl alone. Some fish may nibble the salamander or simply stress it out.

8. Place adult axolotls together with juveniles or babies

If you want to keep more than one axolotl in the same environment, ensure that all animals are the same size. Otherwise, accidents such as bites and even cannibalism can occur.

9. Use water conditioners with Aloe vera

These salamanders, as we discussed several times, are sensitive to some aspects of the water; Aloe vera has a compound that can cause intoxication in your pet.

10. Feed it with hard-shelled animals (snails, super and mealworms)

Feeding axolotls hard-shelled animals like snails or mealworms can lead to intestinal impaction or other digestive problems. The intestinal apparatus of salamanders will not always consume calcareous or chitinous shells present in these worms and snails.

Do you like the book so far?

Hey! Sorry to interrupt. I just wanted to check in and ask if you're enjoying *Axolotl Care Guide* so far? I can't wait to hear what you think of it!

We would be incredibly grateful if you could leave a picture review on Amazon. If you can't leave a picture review, then even a text review of 1 or 2 sentences would mean a whole lot to us.

To do it, go to your amazon shopping app on your phone, click on that. Once you are inside, click on the top three bars in the left-hand corner and click on "your orders."

From there, you'll be able to see what you've bought. Next, scroll down to the item on which you want to leave a picture review, then click "write a product review."

Once there, select how many stars you want to leave and click the book cover. Then click on the camera icon to add a photo or a video; from there, you can take a picture of the book, click on use photo, and then that photo will be uploaded to your amazon app immediately.

Finally, give it a title and write a little bit of text about what you liked about the book.

Reviews are the best way for small authors – like ours – to get noticed and reach a wider audience. For this reason, your support really does make a difference.

CHAPTER 3

FEEDING YOUR AXOLOTLS

A FTER YOU HAVE set up the perfect environment for your amphibian pet, you must consider another crucial part of maintaining these animals: food. There is no secret to feeding these animals and keeping them healthy and at their ideal weight. However, these tips will help a lot, especially if you're a first-time keeper. In this chapter, you will learn what your axolotl eats, the best way to feed them, and how to deal with some feeding problems.

Let's go!

What do axolotls eat in the wild?

These animals come out to feed after sunset. They use their sense of smell and chemical receptors to find food. Because they have such small teeth, the axolotl cannot chew, so it cannot crush its prey but instead swallows it whole, after capturing it using a sucking motion. These amphibians are considered carnivores. In the wild, they feed on anything that moves and fits in their mouth.

In their natural environment, the diet of juvenile axolotls are omnivores, so their diet consists of organic matter, roots, seeds, plant leaves, algae, Daphnia and rotifers, in addition to small crustaceans such as amphipods and isopods, insects, leeches, snails, and small fish. Adult axolotls, however, are strict carnivores and feed primarily on worms, insects, crustaceans, molluscs and some small fish.

What to feed axolotls in captivity

These tiny aquatic animals are known for being gluttons, which is helpful when it comes to feeding them in an aquarium. In addition, they eat a wide range of foods, from live prey to commercial pet food. In captivity, feeding is crucial to maintain the well-being of this salamander. Maintaining the diversity of foods offered is necessary to satisfactorily meet their body's metabolic needs.

It's very important to offer an axolotl food of a size consistent with their mouth. We have already learned that because they feed by suction, they can eat rocks and gravel from the substrate, causing intestinal impaction. That's why we should always use sand, large rocks, or no substrate in their tank.

The same can happen with very large foods. Impaction can also occur with foods like insects and larvae with a rigid exoskeleton, such as crickets, cockroaches, and mealworms, when these are offered regularly. Impaction can also happen when you have too many snails in the tank, and the axolotl eats some of them. These shells, rich in chitin, can irritate the salamander's digestive system, so don't use them as a daily food base. A good rule of thumb is to offer only food smaller than the size of their head. Impaction is a serious problem, in which the main symptom is that your pet has a swollen abdomen and does not defecate. This condition can be fatal.

In addition to the food itself, you must keep an eye on the correct amount and frequency, always trying to maintain the quality of the water and the development, growth, and reproduction of your lovely pet.

Excess food can cause obesity or change the properties of the water if the animal does not consume it entirely. The main foods you can offer your axolotl include brine shrimp, Tubifex, bloodworms, Daphnias, earthworms, fish pellets, frozen bloodworms, and live small fish. Use caution and care when feeding insects such as mealworms, shrimp, cockroaches, and crickets. The ideal is to include as much variety as possible.

Food in relation to age

As mentioned earlier, the diet of axolotls is also directly related to their age—both the type of food and the number of times they feed. Juveniles have a very different diet from adults. So you have to think mainly about the diminutive size of the larvae and the ease of accessing food. In addition, young animals have more significant energy needs, as they need to grow quickly and constantly look for predators.

After birth, they are attached to a yolk sac, which will nourish them for a short period, usually 24 hours. From the larval stage, these amphibians are already hunters. Still, they also present as opportunists, feeding on plant material and decomposing organic matter. When in captivity, after one day from hatching until their first month of life, you can offer them small live foods, such as brine shrimp or Daphnia/Moina nauplii (water fleas). They also accept many small worms, such as microworms and vinegar eels.

It is essential to use live food. In aquariums, these babies will not accept anything that does not move. At this larval stage, they require more than one daily meal. Because they don't have food reserves, the younglings cannot go without, food, or else they will perish. A good tip is always to keep some small Daphnia nauplii or even infusoria (minute freshwater organisms) in your aquarium. You will be able to see how their little bellies are full and reddish after eating.

The exact change in the color of their belly is an excellent thermometer for knowing when they are fed or need to eat again. From the fourth week onward, your pet should already have complete front legs and almost complete hind legs. From then on, the diet is almost the same as it is for adults. At this stage, they still eat daily, but you should keep an eye out if they're refusing food or looking thin. Ideally, their belly should always be the same width as their head.

If the belly is wider than the head, your axolotl is obese. If it's thinner than its head, the animal is too thin. This rule will also be valid for adult animals. As discussed earlier, you should also keep an eye on its poop. Make sure it's defecating and that the feces look healthy. Here you can start offering them adult Daphnias and brine shrimp without any problems, and blackworms and earthworms cut into pieces. You can also provide them with fish fingerlings as a snack. When your salamander reaches a size of more than three inches in length, you can maintain the same diet you would if they were an adult, but you should still feed them daily.

At this point, you can introduce static foods like fresh, frozen, or commercial pet food. In addition to starting to offer them pellets for carnivorous fish - preferably those that sink and those in the shape of a comma, which, when in contact with water, imitate the movement of worms - there are also commercial foods suitable for axolotls, and fresh and frozen foods such as shrimp chunks or bloodworms.

You can also use dry foods like krill, Gammarus, and Tubifex as a snack. However, before offering dry food, leave it in the water to help moisten it. You can also offer some pastes and gels to your animals, but these make the water dirty. Perform a good water change after feeding these foods.

You can use all species of earthworms or live foods, and axolotls will accept most of them well. Some, like red wigglers, can secrete a bitter-tasting substance, so not all salamanders will accept them. Some keepers say that blanching these worms helps with this taste.

Believe it or not, some axolotls are good at exhibiting their food preferences. Just remember to only offer food as large as their head. Small shrimp and mealworms can be used in small portions as a treat. If your pet doesn't defecate right after eating these foods or has strange poop, don't offer them anymore.

When it reaches above nine inches in length, you have an almost adult animal, so you should reduce the feeding frequency to every other day. The width of the belly being about the same as the head remains a good tip. These animals will already eat practically everything you offer them, so if you have started introducing static foods, you should have no problem following an easy-to-obtain, varied, balanced diet. As a staple diet, I recommend earthworms. They are extremely nutritious, with a high content of minerals, proteins, and especially amino acids. Best of all, you can easily produce them in your home, even in small spaces. There are several species of earthworms in different sizes; some will definitely be perfect for your pet axolotl.

It is important to have good quality food for daily use, such as pellets suitable for axolotls or even some gel food. To maintain a varied diet, you should offer them snacks regularly. Bloodworms, Tubifex, frozen shrimp pieces, small live fish, mealworms (be sure to remove the head), and live shrimp are great choices. They are nutritious and readily accepted by the axolotl.

Some axolotl keepers even offer pieces of oily fish, like salmon and sardines. This type of food is not a problem if you maintain a balanced and varied diet. The big issue is that when using this type of food, the water quality drops considerably, so if you decide to add oily fish to your axolotl's diet, immediately proceed with an extensive partial water change. If its diet is deficient, this food can simultaneously make the animal anemic and obese. Moreover, fish pieces are not very nutritious; these amphibians must eat small fish whole, with cartilage, bones, and organs.

Consider buying frozen feeder fish and offering this instead of larger fish pieces. If you use live fish or shrimp to feed your salamander, ensure it comes from a place you know, with good sanitary and handling practices, to avoid contamination in your animals. Ideally, you should quarantine them for a time, to be sure they don't carry any disease.

How to feed an axolotl

Novice keepers may wonder about the best way to feed their pet axolotl. It's not complicated, but let's review some tips that can help you, especially when offering non-live food the first few times. As we have discussed many times by now, axolotls feed using a sucking motion. Unfortunately, they don't have excellent eyesight, so the first step is always to offer food right in front of them and at the height of their mouths.

With live food, this is easy, since the axolotl - in addition to chemically sensing that the food is there - can see movement. In the case of live fish or shrimp, as incredible as it may seem, these animals are excellent hunters and will chase their prey until they eat them. Consider purchasing a pair of long tweezers, though be careful to choose a model without sharp edges that could hurt your salamander.

It is easier to direct the food with the tweezers. Just hold bloodworms or mealworms, for example, in the clamp in front of the amphibian, and it will take care of the rest. Earthworms move and slowly sink, so if you put them close to the axolotl, it will feed quickly.

Remember the importance of offering food that is the correct size. If your amphibian appears fearful or apprehensive at feeding time, try offering smaller-sized foods. You can always cut the worms. When using the tweezers, be careful not to bump or let the food hit your axolotl's gills; these are very sensitive and are easily hurt. If using commercial food, throw the pellet or paste directly in front of the animal. If it doesn't catch it, remove the leftovers immediately.

The food factor is intrinsically linked to the water quality of aquariums. Overfeeding your animals causes them to excrete more toxic substances into the water, degrading the water quality. In addition, if the axolotl is given too much and doesn't feed on all of it, leftovers that remain in the tank will decay, spoiling the water in the home of your aquatic friend. That's why it's important to remove any uneaten food from the tank.

There are instruments that can help you do this, like pipettes (especially those for feeding corals), siphons, or even a turkey baster. With these items, you can remove bits and pieces of food (as well as poop) from a specific part of the aquarium.

The water can also become oily and dyed when you feed oily fish pieces, homemade pastes, gels, or low-quality pet food. If you use any of these foods, do a significant water change immediately to ensure the water in your aquarium is clean and your pet is happy and well-fed.

Frequency of feeding – How often should an axolotl be fed?

As we discussed earlier, this depends on the stage of development of your axolotl. Generally speaking, juveniles should be fed daily, and adults every two or three days. Just like most animals, a young axolotl needs to be fed constantly. Remember that it is in the growth and development phase, so it requires significant energy to fully develop.

Remember, if your axolotl's abdomen is distended and red, it is well-fed, so you can wait a little before offering more food. On the other hand, if you notice an empty, whitish belly, feed it. If you always keep live food in your aquarium, you can be confident that your animals will always have a full stomach, and you won't need to worry that they are eating enough.

In the first week of life, offer food two to three times a day, especially in the morning. Never stop feeding salamanders at this age. Unlike adults, they will die in a few days if they don't have food. As your pet grows, you can gradually decrease the frequency of feeding. When the food inside their stomach is no longer visible, use the head-to-belly size ratio rule, since this will tell you whether you need to feed more or less.

Adult axolotls have a prolonged metabolism, which means their digestion is long. Therefore, I strongly recommend feeding them every two or three days. Some keepers feed them daily, but I do not recommend this practice because it could make them obese, and could also speed up their metabolism, causing them to live shorter lives.

Overfeeding can also cause bowel problems like gas, constipation, impaction, and other issues. When keeping animals in captivity, it is crucial to keep in mind consistency and balance, so our animals are at the ideal weight for their stage of life.

Create a routine for feeding your axolotl. Discipline is one of the most beneficial characteristics in anyone who wishes to have an aquarium and a healthy animal.

Foods to avoid

For starters, avoid unknown food or food with a dubious origin, such as animals collected in polluted places or otherwise not properly quarantined. In addition to having diseases and parasites, these can kill your axolotl by carrying toxic elements like pesticides and other pollutants.

Always buy live foods from farms and breeders that you know are of good quality. Those raised in optimal conditions already have some treatment or prior quarantine. Adult axolotls do not feed on plant foods. In nature, young individuals need a small percentage (from 12 to 20 percent of their total diet) of plant material, but this does not occur in aquariums. Never offer vegetables or commercial herbivore foods to these amphibians. If your axolotls are eating pieces of aquarium plants, it is because they are hungry or stressed, so find out what the cause is and solve the problem.

Inert food should not be their only food base. Pellets do not offer everything these animals need to be strong and healthy, especially if they are in the growth phase. Therefore, take care to provide a varied diet consisting of commercial, live, and fresh foods.

Avoid offering hard shell worms, bugs, or toxic prey like beetles, centipedes, etc. The same goes for foods like Alabama jumpers, red wigglers, dried shrimp, and mealworms. These can be offered occasionally, as long as your pet is receiving a balanced diet. In addition to causing gastric problems, the protein utilization of these animals is very low because the salamander's stomach has to expend more energy digesting the shell than absorbing the nutrients.

Axolotl foods that you can raise at home

As we've seen, live food for your axolotl is vital for any keeper. This is the most natural way of feeding and increases their vitality, allowing them to hunt as they do in their habitat. In addition, it provides them with a balanced and varied diet. However, the variety of live food is enormous. Luckily, the vast majority of it can be produced at home, simply and efficiently.

Brine shrimp

Artemias are crustaceans often given as food. Therefore, their nauplii (larval stage) are extremely important. Their size goes up to one inch. Eggs are relatively easy to store, as they can be kept dry for a long time. They depend on saline water to live well and constantly produce eggs. They are easy to acquire and you can even find pre-assembled kits to maintain your own brine shrimp factory.

Daphnias, Moinas and Ostracodas

These are very similar to brine shrimp. The only difference is that they live in fresh water, and the eggs do not need to go through a dry period. Just build a tank for them, provide infusorians as food, and that's it; you have an endless supply of these nutritious animals.

Vinegar worms (Turbatrix aceti)

Vinegar worms, about 1-2 millimeters (approximately half an inch) in diameter, are a relatively minor type of live food. They are particularly suitable for the larval and juvenile stages of salamanders. These worms swim freely in the water. To maintain and multiply them, fill a container with 5-6 percent household vinegar, which you can also mix with water (maximum ratio 1:1). Add a teaspoon of sugar and a small amount of dry yeast per liter of vinegar. The preparation must be shaken regularly and must not be completely sealed.

Grindal worms

Grindal worms belong to the ringworm family, as do earthworms, which are their large relatives. This is a highly sought-after and simple live food species that, if handled properly, provides enough nourishment for a long time. The small white worms, about one centimeter (less than half an inch) long, are very high in fat and protein.

Earthworms

Among the many types of live food, one stands out for its nutritional characteristics - earthworms. Thousands of species are found around the world. These can be used in practically all stages of an amphibian's life, and they have countless other attributes. Earthworms would undoubtedly be considered pests if they weren't so beneficial to nature. Every two months, they double their population, a good attribute for the breeders of these annelids.

But the benefits do not stop there: earthworms improve the quality of the soil, serve as food, and can even be an extra income since they are in high demand in the market. Small and long, the worms penetrate the earth and, with their movements, revolve, aerate and unpack the soil, preventing waterlogging and reducing erosion.

At the same time, in their digestive process, they eliminate decomposing remains and "clean" the soil, returning a natural fertilizer to the environment. This is called humus and is great for developing vegetables, fruit trees, and other crops. Rich in protein, earthworms are a good food option for many animals.

Another vital role of earthworms is in the elimination of household organic waste. Fun fact: earthworms do not have eyes, teeth, or bones, but they can regrow a new tail.

What is worm farming?

The demand for earthworms for use as animal food has increased in recent years. But many aquarists live in large cities, and it is challenging to find earthworms, so creating them is an excellent option.

Farming is simple, cheap, and does not require significant maintenance. There are a few setup mounts for farming these worms. The worm farm with stacked boxes is the most practical option for those living in apartments or houses without a yard. It is easy to find templates on the internet that are already assembled for you to start using. For do-it-yourselfers, however, it's not difficult to assemble your own.

How to set up a worm farm at home

With enough space, you can set up a worm farm that can even be a source of income.

1. **Start** - Begin with a few worms. Place 2 to 3 gallons of worms in a 6.5-square-foot bed.
2. **Expansion** - For larger productions, use a 6.5 x 3.5-foot bed, 1 foot deep. Deposit 19 cubic feet of tanned manure.
3. **Environment** - The worm farm must be kept clean to prevent predators from invading. Dry straw on top will inhibit activity of birds. Remove any grass

around the bed so there is no seed contamination. Do not let the number of worms become excessive, and there should not be variations in humidity and temperature, as they do not like very hot places.

4. **Structure** - Install your worm farm above ground level and on a level area, but with a slight slope to prevent water accumulation., The walls should be made of masonry or wood and have drains to drain excess moisture. Protect the site from the rain with plastic screens supported on wire, bamboo, or wooden supports.

5. **Feeding** - Earthworms feed on manure and plant debris, such as grass, fruit, dry leaves, paper, and decaying organic matter. Put it all together to make compost. Make a 3-foot-tall mound in a cool, dry place. Let it rest for a week, and turn the material over to increase aeration. Repeat the procedure only with one turn until the compost cools down. Take the mixture to the worm bed and squeeze a handful to make sure it doesn't drip water, which means it's ready for feeding.

6. **Reproduction** - Despite being hermaphrodites (having both male and female reproductive organs), earthworms do not self-fertilize. Therefore, mating with another earthworm is required, which can take place all year round. Fertilized and inside a cocoon, the eggs are expelled into the earth. They hatch in about 21 days, and each gives rise to a few little worms.

7. **Harvesting** - The trap method is one of the best techniques to collect the worms produced. Fill burlap sacks with wet, weathered manure, spreading them over the bed to attract worms. After capturing most of them, transfer them wherever you want.

How to set up a worm bin at home

To be clear: the composter worm has no smell and is not disgusting when well cared for. The worms are calm inside the box, and the compost looks like dark and fluffy earth.

1. **Size your composter:**

The size and number of boxes largely depend on the number of people living in your house. Organic waste takes, on average, 45 days to be transformed into compost. Thus, you must calculate composting cycles that include the number of food scraps and the dry matter. It is crucial to maintain a balance. For example, in more humid environments, decomposition happens faster, but bad smells are a risk. In very dry places, decomposition takes much longer. Unfortunately, earthworms suffer from both extremes.

The standard is between 20 and 30 parts of dry matter to one of wet material. In the end, the volume decreases, with a 10 to 1 ratio in the humus. You must use at least three boxes. One is lower to collect the liquid slurry, and another is to make the rotation. As you fill one, the worms eat the other. When the second fills up, you empty the first.

Use two 10-gallon boxes to produce 4.5 lbs. of plant waste (the average for a family of four) per day. Adjust the proportion for the size of your boxes and the amount of garbage.

2. **What you will need to assemble your worm composter:**

I. Plastic boxes with lids that, when stacked, fit securely. You can use any container as long as it is not transparent. They serve as organization boxes or canning buckets;

II. Tap for filter;

III. Some soil, such as earth or worm cast;

IV. Earthworms. There are many earthworm species. Choose the one that best suits you. Aquarists routinely use Himalayan Violet and Californian Red. If you can't find live worms to buy, the humus is full of worm eggs. It takes a little longer, but soon they appear in your compost bin;

V. Dry organic material. It could be grass clippings, dry leaves you collect near your home, or sawdust (it mustn't contain any chemicals like paint or varnish).

3. How to assemble:

I. Drill several small holes in the two boxes to receive the waste. They must be small enough so the humus doesn't run all the way into the boxes below but big enough for the worms to move through. From 1-1.5 millimeters will work.

II. In the lower box, intended for fertilizer slurry collection, make a hole on the side so the faucet can be fitted and installed. That's where your liquid fertilizer will come from. To avoid clogging, you can add a screen on the inside.

III. Make a bed with earthworm humus in the first digester box after the one destined for the slurry. It will be the first to receive food, kicking off the system. If you have worms, you can put them there too.

Ready! Now start composting your organic waste. Constantly monitor the situation of the composter, adding dry matter when you notice something is not going well there. Whenever possible, mix the compost so that air enters and encourages aerobic decomposition, carried out by bacteria that will do much of the work for you. When the material formed is uniform and practically odorless, it is ready for you to collect the worm cast.

If you don't have a place to put the fertilizer and slurry afterward, give it to someone or to the plants in a nearby park. The top container of your worm bin must always be covered, and there must be no gaps between the different floors. Otherwise, the worms could escape.

4. What can and can't be put in the compost bin:
Everything you put in your organic compost bin sooner or later will decompose. There is nothing prohibited. But remember, balance is critical. Earthworms don't like to live in a very acidic environment, so it's good to use citrus compounds, such as orange and lemon peels, in moderation. Acidity can also attract other less desirable animals, such as wasps and some types of flies. The same goes for meat, dairy, and cooked foods. Very slow decomposition can cause a foul smell and attract unwanted insects. So avoid this as much as possible. Paper and cardboard are welcome but without any paint or varnish.

How to catch worms from your garden
Collecting earthworms from a garden is simple, especially after a good rain on a hot day. After the rain, the annelids are closer to the surface, mainly in the litter layer on the ground, which facilitates their capture. It's important to find a garden without chemical treatment, garbage, or any pollutants. Then, make sure the worms are of excellent quality.

You can use some trap or actively capture them using a shovel. Use starchy vegetables like carrots, beets, or potatoes to attract them. Just put it in direct contact with the ground and wait a few minutes. When you go back and lift the piece of vegetable, you will find many worms stuck to it and underneath it. Use the shovel to dig in different places and pick up the worms you find.

How to store your worms

Most of the time, you will hardly buy your axolotl's food in the exact amount you need, which means you'll have to keep this food alive. Some food you can freeze, but with different worms, this is impossible; you must keep them alive until you use them as food. Blackworms are one of the easiest, and you can keep them for up to four weeks without any problems. First, put them in a jar (with a lid) with a bit of water, then store them in the fridge.

Among night crawlers, only the Canadian ones can be kept in the fridge; they must be kept dry. Other night crawlers, like red wigglers, European, and African, should be kept the same way as earthworms. A bucket of soil or other substrate and organic material to feed them works well. It's a good idea to have a worm bin, one for each species.

FAQs about feeding

Q1 Why does my axolotl refuse to eat worms?

This is not normal behavior, as earthworms are one of the favorite foods of these animals. The first thing you should do is determine whether your axolotl is in good physical condition and if everything is okay with it. The second is to check and test the different aquarium water parameters. Salamanders will refuse to eat when kept in poor water quality or suboptimal standards. After correcting the problem, they will continue with their usual diet.

Another factor may be the species of earthworm used, as in the case of red wigglers, which secrete substances that are not so palatable. In this case, you can blanch the worms before offering them to your pet or simply provide another species of worms as food.

Q2 How long can I leave food in my axolotl's tank?

This is a question worth talking about over and over again. Feeding them too much can harm their health. The problem is serious because the animal can become obese. Another point to note is that when an axolotl overeats, he tends to dirty the water more through his excreta. This will also lead to rapid water quality degradation.

Leftovers should be avoided as much as possible, as they can harm the quality of the water, which will then require replacement, along with cleaning the aquarium and filter more often. If there are leftovers, they must be removed as soon as possible with a mesh, sieve, turkey baster, pipette, or siphon so they do not dissolve and spoil the water.

Feeding your axolotl correctly is very important for their development and quality of life because, as we have seen in this chapter, excess food can intoxicate the water and even cause the death of your pet. But feeding these animals is quite simple. The key is to keep an eye on the size of the food offered and the life stage of your axolotl.

To keep your salamander healthy, you must maintain a balanced and varied diet. A range of foods can be easily kept and reproduced in your home. Owning and caring for these foods is almost as fun as keeping axolotls, and it helps you recycle food scraps and even earn extra income.

This concludes our chapter on how to feed your axolotl. In the next chapter we'll discuss how to address health issues. Though keeping these pets is fairly straightforward, sometimes problems emerge, and you must know how to deal with them.

CHAPTER 4

HEALTH ISSUES WITH AXOLOTLS

I N THE PREVIOUS chapters, we discussed how to correctly keep an axolotl. Now I will talk about another important part of maintaining these animals: how to notice and deal with diseases and other conditions. No matter how careful you are with your pet, illnesses can happen. Knowing how to diagnose and treat quickly is essential when keeping animals. The speed with which you respond to the first symptoms will make the difference in the treatment and cure of your salamander.

First of all, keep in mind that I am not a veterinarian, just someone with extensive knowledge of keeping axolotls as pets. But in my long journey, I've dealt with several health issues related to these animals. This chapter will serve as a guide to help you diagnose the main problems that these salamanders suffer in aquariums. While I offer several tips to diagnose problems here, I must tell you that as soon as you notice something wrong, please be sure to immediately take your amphibian to a specialized veterinarian. Only a vet can provide the correct diagnosis and effective and safe treatment for your beloved pet.

You should never use treatments found on internet pages and in videos. These bare-skinned amphibians are fragile and susceptible to medications and water changes; any rough treatment could be fatal. Many diseases that attack axolotls have similar symptoms, so as simple as an accurate diagnosis may seem, it is not. Several factors, from some water parameters to the genetics of an individual, can make diagnosis difficult, even by experienced breeders.

If you don't already have a specialized vet, you should be able to find a professional online who will have the extensive knowledge and experience to treat your axolotl. Always turn to these professionals. Many say specialized treatment can be expensive, complicated, and time-consuming, but if you do not have the time or financial resources for such treatment, I advise you not to keep these animals. When we decide to get a pet, we make a commitment and take responsibility to offer them the same care we would offer our children: a quality environment, nutritious food, and medical treatment.

What's the first thing to do?

First, you should know that axolotls that are fed correctly, with a balanced diet, and that are in good and stable water conditions, are unlikely to become sick. Diseases can come in two ways: the first is that there has been some variation in the parameters in the tank of these animals, such as your chiller stopping working on a hot day or the pH dropping sharply due to inadequate maintenance. That's why I reinforce the need for constant water chemistry measurements and always having meters for physical parameters like water temperature.

The second way diseases get in is by contamination. In previous chapters, we talked about the importance of quarantining new individuals and live foods. It is also crucial that you take care of the nets and the equipment used for water exchange. Avoid using the same equipment in multiple aquariums. If you do, sanitize it correctly with a hypersaline solution (water with a lot of salt) and exposure to light and heat (sun).

Avoiding illness is always the ideal. But we know that sometimes, even with great care, things happen. Know your animals and always be aware of their behavior, so you will quickly notice any aberrant behavior. This is the key to the rapid treatment and healing of any animal.

Checking and correcting parameters

If you notice that your pet is showing signs of disease, you should take action quickly. The first thing to do, without any doubt, is to check the aquarium equipment, like light intensity, and check if the temperature controllers and filter are working correctly.

Then measure the aquarium parameters pH, oxygen in the water, ammonia, nitrite, nitrate, temperature, and whatever else you can.

The parameters that your aquarium must demonstrate in the tests are:

- Temperature: about 63°F (or 15-18°C)

- Ammonia: 0

- Nitrite: 0

- Nitrate: below 7

- pH: about 7.5

- KH: 3-8

- GH: 7-14

- Oxygen: 70-100 percent

- Salinity: 0

- Axolotl's Mood: Happy

Whenever you touch your aquarium, ensure your hands and arms are clean and free from perfume, lotion, or soap residue; these things can be fatal to amphibians. After the measurements, write down the results and compare them with the results of your last measurements. This step shows the importance of having your tests always written down. **To keep your measurements up to date, you can also use the freebie bonus #2 the Axolotl care log.** That way, you can compare and figure out if something has become unbalanced.

If anything is wrong, be sure to perform a significant water change, correct the parameters, and clean and readjust the equipment. This is the first action you should take. The next day, repeat the tests and see if everything remains stable. If in doubt, check chapter 2 of this book for the ideal maintenance parameters, how to perform correct maintenance, and the necessary tests.

While you take care of the aquarium, cleaning, and testing, isolate your axolotl in small hospital containers, which we call an "axolotl tub" or just a "tub."

How do I tub my axolotl?

This tub is nothing more than a small space container where your axolotl will remain stress-free. In the tub, you must perform total water changes - the more times a day, the better. That's the main reason to use small-space containers. You must pay attention to the fact that these animals cannot withstand sudden temperature changes, so the new water must have the same physical and chemical parameters as the water you remove.

A tip is to keep a good amount of water, like a gallon, inside some type of container, and keep it close to where you placed your tub, so both will be at the same temperature. The water will have the same standards if they come from the same source. You can use either spring water or tap water. If using tap water, always use a high-quality water conditioner.

Usually, the size of the tub should be no more than four gallons. This size makes it easy to clean, perform water changes, and move, if necessary, though it would be best if you do not move it. Another tip is to use non-transparent materials, to minimize the external stimuli that your salamander receives.

You can improve the tub by adding hiding places and an aerator. Remember to keep few bubbles going per minute; strong disturbances can stress your pet even more. The parameters must be close to the ideal; again, check the standards necessary to maintain an axolotl in chapter 2 of this book. Remember, axolotls can jump, so keep a lid or a space between the surface of the water and the outer edge of your tub.

Verifying tank maintenance

For stable maintenance of the optimal parameters of your axolotl tank, you must perform good maintenance and cleaning practices on your tank. One of the causes of illness is that you've missed an important step or have done it wrong. The beneficial bacteria mainly help the stability of a tank's water quality in filters, substrates, and on practically all aquarium surfaces. But these bacteria can become fragile under some circumstances. Remember to never use tap water without treating it with a water conditioner suitable for an aquarium. The elements in the water, such as chlorine and chloramine, are toxic to your salamander and reduce the population of the beneficial bacteria.

Good conditioners also remove heavy metals, among other things, so you should always use a good quality one, as these elements are harmful to your tank and the animals that live there. When your aquarium's bacteria suffer some loss, it's as if it isn't cycling. The levels of nitrogenous compounds will be high, and you will have to cycle your tank again.

The same occurs with aquariums that need to be adequately cleaned. You should always siphon the substrate or the aquarium floor, removing all dirt. Do this during your weekly water change. Change at least 30 percent of the aquarium water. Contrary to what some say, there are no limits to water exchange as long as the new water is within the aquarium's general parameters. But changing little water is very harmful.

Clean the decorations and your filter every two to four weeks. Disassemble the filter and rinse the media, sponges, and other filter elements, constantly changing the activated carbon and resins (if you use them). It is imperative to carry out this cleaning only with the water you removed from the aquarium or with water treated with conditioner. Dirt in the aquarium or the filter, if not cleaned and removed, will accumulate and deteriorate the quality of the water, raising the levels of ammonia and decreasing the pH of the water. That's why cleaning is so important.

After performing maintenance, ensure that you have reconnected the equipment and that everything is working perfectly.

Examining tank environment

The environment is crucial; you must always pay attention to what you put in your aquariums, which is why paying attention during the moment of assembly is so important. Being informed about the use of only safe materials for your aquarium and axolotl is critical to avoid problems.

Regarding the tank environment, keep an eye on the quality and origin of the decorations that you're using, especially if they have edges that could hurt the salamander's thin and sensitive skin or if they are not decorations suitable for an aquarium, since these can release ink and other toxic elements into the water. If you choose to use substrate, remember that axolotls can eat gravel and sand that is not fine enough, which causes several digestive problems. Therefore, always use extremely thin substrates or those larger than the animal's head.

Choosing the wrong tank mates can lead to accidents as well. Do not place your axolotl with aggressive fish, smaller or larger axolotls, or animals that the amphibian could eat or that will nip the axolotl.

Common problems: Symptoms and treatment suggestions

Axolotls demonstrate that they are not doing well through behavioral signs that we can notice through observation. Likewise, solid physical symptoms we can see in the amphibian's body will help us know what is wrong with our pet. Observing any changes can help identify some diseases. Changes differ according to the illness's cause: trauma, fungi, bacteria, or parasites.

Among the most common changes due to problems are:

- Skin lesions (wounds, bruises, stains, blisters, lumps, abscesses, strange appearance, etc.);

- Apathy;

- Lack of appetite;

- Bruised or strange gills, tail, or other parts of the body;

- Tail with abnormal appearance;

- Swollen abdomen;

- Excessive mucus on the skin;

- Abnormal buoyancy;

- Sighing or swallowing when not eating;

- Not being able to close the mouth;

- Scratching/rubbing against substrate or objects in the aquarium;

- Going up in search of air (pulmonary breathing);

- Decreased size of gills;

- Dull or asymmetrical eyes;

- Cessation of growth.

As much as these anomalies give us a way forward to find out what's wrong with our aquatic friend, they're only part of the puzzle. When proceeding with the diagnosis, we must determine everything that happened in its environment, the state the animal was and is in, and everything else we can know. Only then will we know what is wrong. Accurate diagnosis is not always easy, so taking your animal directly to a trusted veterinarian is recommended as soon as the first sign of illness is detected.

On the other hand, some behaviors are normal or simply signal that something in the tank is incorrect—not something to be concerned about but that requires close observation on your part.

Floating

Floating close to the surface of the water is something that many axolotls do, in other words, expected behavior. However, when done excessively or when your animal is visibly having trouble returning to the bottom of the aquarium, this is a sign that something is wrong. Some agents cause these disorders. For example, digestive problems like gas, impaction, constipation, and inaccurate water temperature can cause your axolotl to float on the surface.

In the case of the wrong temperature, lower and stabilize the temperature, and your axolotl will return to normal.

The same will occur with gas (bloating) or constipation; after a while or after the animal defecates, it will return to normal. If the behavior persists for more than two days, and it stops accepting food and defecating, you are probably dealing with an impaction.

Possible treatment

Check and correct the water parameters and perform cleaning and a water change. Avoid feeding the axolotl while it is floating, but you can offer small amounts of food to see if it accepts or rejects it. Isolating your axolotl in a tub until it gets better is a good idea, to avoid causing even more stress to the animal. You can also use the technique known as "fridging," which is nothing more than placing your salamander in a tub with a temperature of 40°F. This is a harsh treatment and should only be used in severe cases.

Ways to prevent

I know I'm repeating a few things here, but these are very important points that can't be said too often. Obviously, preventing problems is much easier than fixing them. So take care to only offer your salamander food about the size of its head. Do not use substrates or decorations in the aquarium that can be swallowed, such as small stones and gravel. Avoid snails which, when eaten, can cause constipation. Offer hard shell insects only rarely, since they can also cause impaction. It is recommended to keep these amphibians alone in a tank, because they can eat relatively large fish, which causes problems.

White cotton growth on gills or limbs

If you notice a growth or fluffy substance on the skin of your animal or even discoloration, it has been affected by fungus. These signs can accompany other symptoms, such as the salamander scratching itself in different places in the tank. Fungus is an evil directly linked to poor water quality.

Possible treatment
It is worth noting that there are several types of chemical treatment available, but you should only use them with the consent and help of a specialized veterinarian. It is also important to say that no matter how actively you treat the fungus, the disease will remain and return in your axolotl if you don't keep the aquarium water in excellent condition. You might also add Indian almond leaves, which have mild anti-fungal properties, directly in the tank. The best treatment for fungus is to keep the water of excellent quality and the environment always clean. When these factors are controlled, the fungus will disappear.

Ways to prevent
Always keep the water in excellent quality and its maintenance up to date.

Bacterial infections

Diseases caused by bacteria are serious and must be treated quickly. In addition, they are always associated with poor water quality. The main symptoms are the surface of the axolotl's body showing red spots or ulcers, lack of appetite, and even bleeding.

Possible treatment

You must bring your axolotl to a veterinarian so they can administer antibiotic medications.

Ways to prevent

Maintaining good quality and hygiene in the environment is essential to avoid bacterial diseases.

Wounds and injuries

If you notice any bruises or cuts on your animal's body, whether or not they're accompanied by bleeding, these injuries are caused by direct trauma, such as getting a gill stuck at the entrance of the filter or by being attacked by other animals.

Possible treatment

Keep the water in the axolotl tank at optimal quality until the animal heals to avoid the entry of fungi and bacteria. You can use Indian almond leaves for their bactericidal power. The pH must be controlled when using these leaves, however, as the water tends to acidify.

Ways to prevent

Keep your animals alone or with other axolotls of equal size. Do not use decorations that could cut or injure your salamander.

Bent gills or folded tail

If your axolotl's gills are bent or droopy, it is a clear sign that they are suffering from stress. However, if the problem is only in the tail, look for other symptoms, as it may be another disease, in addition to stress. Other symptoms of stress are aberrant swimming and squirming slightly. When stressed, these animals stop eating, which makes them weak and inhibits their immune system.

Possible treatment
Perform a water test, and proceed with an extensive water change and tank cleaning to stabilize the parameters.

Ways to prevent
Keep up your regular maintenance and testing to certify the water quality.

Spinning & balancing problems

Salamanders often do this; if you notice these things more frequently, you should be concerned, since it is probably a neurological problem.

Possible treatment
Immediately take your animal to the vet; only a professional will be able to conduct tests and determine the cause of this behavior and the appropriate treatment.

Ways to prevent
This condition can be genetic, so my advice is to always purchase your animals from reputable and respected breeders. Keeping the water in top condition will also prevent your animal from being infected by bacteria that will attack its brain.

Thrashing around

Maybe you notice your salamander is visibly annoyed, lunging at the glass or decorations. It is bizarre behavior and challenging to understand what is happening. This behavior can have multiple causes, ranging from external parasites, the animal having aggression issues, or neurological problems.

Possible treatment
Isolate the animal in a tub, carry out the tests in the aquarium water and visually look for any changes in their body. If nothing is found and the behavior persists, speak to your vet.

Ways to prevent
Keep the water in good quality, the aquarium free from threats, and the external environment free from stressful stimuli.

Gill kicking

When your axolotl makes the same movement as a dog that scratches its ear with its back paw, this is a clear sign of ammonia in the aquarium water.

Possible treatment
Perform a significant partial water change along with a complete tank cleaning.

Ways to prevent
Keep the water in your axolotl tank always in perfect condition, with tests up to date and well-done weekly maintenance.

Gills turning red/white or falling off

This can be a severe problem. Usually, the gills of these animals change color. When engaging in a lot of activity, they acquire an intense red hue; when axolotls are at rest, they become more whitish.

But when they become very red, this can be a symptom of a bacterial infection, ammonia burning, or low water oxygenation. When they acquire a paler color than usual, it can mean fungal infections or just a signal that your animal is apathetic.

Possible treatment
The first thing to do is carry out an ammonia and an oxygen test and then correct these parameters by changing the water. In case of fungal or bacterial infections, watch for additional symptoms and carry out the treatments we've discussed.

Ways to prevent
Maintaining the optimal quality and oxygenation of your aquarium is essential for your axolotl to live without problems.

Mouth hanging open

An axolotl holds its mouth open for a few reasons. For example, they may have something stuck in their mouth (in which case, they might be opening and closing it), they might have been injured, might have some deformity in their jaw, or could simply be under stress because of poor water quality.

Possible treatment

The first thing to do is to carry out the necessary tests to know the water quality. Then change the water. If you notice something stuck in the animal's mouth, gently, with the help of long tweezers, try to remove it. If it's difficult, take your pet to a vet.

Ways to prevent

Keep the water quality perfect for the salamander and do not leave substrate or decorative objects around that it can swallow. Of course, remember to always offer food smaller than the axolotl's head.

Swelling of neck & limbs/General bloating (swollen belly)

These symptoms occur in multiple conditions: bacterial diseases, intestinal impaction, stress, etc., so watch carefully for other symptoms to arrive at a correct diagnosis.

Possible treatment

As always, the aquarium water must be in perfect condition. The food offered must be of ideal size, and the aquarium must not contain gravel or stones that the axolotl could swallow.

Ways to prevent

Performing water tests and keeping the quality stable and your axolotl fed correctly are the primary preventative measures.

Skin peeling off

Axolotls, like other salamanders, regularly shed the mucus layer that covers their bodies, giving the impression that they are falling apart. The removed layer of mucus is usually eaten, but this is not always the case, and you may even find a layer of slime floating around in the tank.

Some situations can cause your axolotl to produce more mucus than usual – for example, if it is kept at a high temperature. In addition, poor water quality, such as very acidic pH, ammonia, or other substances in the water, can have the same effect of increasing slime production. In advanced-stage fungal infections, the amphibian can be covered entirely by white spots resembling cotton.

Possible treatment
Check if everything is okay in the aquarium, from the environmental characteristics to the water quality. The problems will end when the water is in perfect condition to keep these animals.

Ways to prevent
Never skip weekly maintenance on your aquarium, and perform periodic measurements of pH, ammonia, and temperature.

Refusing to eat or spitting out food

These are signs that by themselves don't mean much, so you have to look at the general condition of your axolotl to know what's really going on with it. For example, it may still be full from its last meal or not want to eat the food you are offering. In any case, not eating is one of the main symptoms of virtually every disease mentioned in this guide and deserves your attention.

Possible treatment
Carefully monitor the general hygiene condition of the aquarium and the water. Carefully watch your axolotl for additional symptoms.

Ways to prevent
The best way to prevent this is to maintain good general care practices for your salamander and aquarium.

Problems with poop

Axolotl poop is like a thermometer. You can use it to know about and measure various aspects of your animal's health.

Why is my axolotl pooping a lot?
This mainly occurs when you overfeed your salamander. Adult axolotls usually defecate only once after each feeding. If your pet is pooping a lot, reduce the food frequency. It's essential to remove poop regularly, as it can quickly degrade water quality.

Why is my axolotl eating poop?
These salamanders have poor eyesight and are incredibly greedy beings; anything moving around them they will eat, even gravel. Eating poop does not usually cause problems for the animal, but it is another reason you should remove their feces.

Why is my axolotl's poop white?

This is a worrisome sign. Most of the time, whitish stool mean your pet has internal parasites. If you see that your animal is defecating white, take it to the vet.

Why is my axolotl poop green?

Green poop occurs in animals with a prolonged digestive system or in those that have not eaten. The green color is from the bile secreted by the animal, and it's nothing to worry about.

Why does my axolotl not poop?

If your axolotl has not defecated for more than four days, isolate it in a tub and offer small-sized food. Note if the animal's abdomen or cloaca is swollen and has other impaction symptoms. After a while in the tub, they should defecate; if not, try fridging them and take them to the vet.

Stringy slime over the mouth and red streaking over the skin

These symptoms are clear signs of a bacterial infection known as columnaris. This disease can be present in aquariums and the animal's body, just waiting for a dip in the animal's immune system that allows the disease to present itself.

Possible treatment

The first thing you should do when you notice the disease is to isolate your animal in a tub and perform a complete water exchange of your aquarium. To end the disease, fridge your amphibian. The bacteria causing this disease die below 53°F. Keep in mind that it is imperative to treat the aquarium. Otherwise, your animal will be reinfested. I strongly recommend visiting a vet as well, so they can see if it is necessary to administer medication.

Ways to prevent
The best form of prevention is to keep your axolotl in a stable environment, free from stress, and with a varied and quality diet.

Typical behavior that is not a health problem

Some behaviors performed by axolotls are entirely normal and nothing to worry about. If you think something is wrong, it is crucial that you observe the frequency of these movements and also note if there are any other associated symptoms. But don't worry; in most cases there is nothing to be concerned about.

Yawning
Axolotls may yawn right after eating or when they have eaten a large amount of food. Yawning acts as a block to the gag reflex.

Axolotls smiling
These salamanders are not exactly smiling, but after swallowing their food, they may have their mouths slightly open, giving the impression that they are smiling.

Zooming around the tank
This happens more in younger axolotls. It's normal and means they're exploring. This behavior can also occur after a water change or when they are startled.

Sitting on top of each other
No one has yet figured out why they do this!

Having difficulty finding food
It is normal behavior that occurs because these animals have very little vision. Nothing to worry about, as most of the time they pick up the location of food through chemical receptors.

Holding still
They are relatively slow metabolism animals, and adult individuals are lazy. Standing at the bottom of the tank is standard behavior. They also hunt by ambush, calmly waiting for prey to pass in front of them.

Flapping gills
They do this to capture more oxygen from the water. In case of frequent movement of the gills, carry out an oxygen test in the water.

Gulping air
Axolotls have rudimentary lungs. It is normal to sometimes rise to the surface and breathe atmospheric air. This occurs most often when the water has a low level of oxygen.

Nose down posture
They assume this position when they're looking for food. It's normal.

In this chapter, we covered topics related to the health of our dear axolotls. As you can see, it all boils down to keeping them in clean aquariums and with the water in ideal and stable parameters - in other words, in excellent condition.

We also learned about the importance of observing your pet's behavior and becoming familiar with it in depth. That way, you'll quickly realize when something is wrong and can work to reverse the situation. None of this is terribly complicated, but be sure to have a vet you trust, and don't hesitate to ask them for help.

In the next chapter, we'll discuss reproduction and breeding of these lovely little animals.

CHAPTER 5

ALL ABOUT BREEDING AXOLOTLS

S O FAR WE'VE learned all the necessary points to keeping an axolotl in perfect conditions, and reviewed problems, diseases, and what to do if they happen. But while keeping these pleasant pets is a wonderful experience, imagine reproducing them!

Animals in captivity only reproduce when they are in perfect health and in a perfect environment. So if you manage to breed your salamanders, congratulations! Your axolotls are healthy and being properly maintained.

Let's now talk about the reproduction of these animals and how you can achieve this in your aquarium.

Determining sex

Axolotls, as previously mentioned, are neotenic animals; that is, they maintain their larval form even after reaching sexually maturity. Axolotl reproduction is not complicated but requires time and dedication, just like so much else in life. After you have your animals well adapted and your aquarium kept in perfect condition, the first step is to know if you have a male and female and if they are ready to mate and produce babies.

Axolotls can be sexually mature from the age of six months, although most reach puberty around a year to a year and a half. Distinguishing between males and females is an easy task after they reach sexual maturity and a specific size. Males have characteristic protuberances at the base of the tail, just behind the cloaca, and are thinner than females. These lumps are sperm deposits and become even more visible during breeding. Females do not have these bumps and tend to have stockier bodies and shorter, wider heads.

Axolotls exhibit a particular mating ritual, which you can use to determine whether your animals are ready to breed. These rituals include body language and chemical communication through pheromones secreted in the male's cloaca.

Breeding season

The breeding season begins in late winter. In the northern hemisphere, it occurs between February and April. In the south, it is from August to November. But spawning can also happen in the middle of summer and winter.

You can breed them practically all year round in captivity, just mimicking natural cold water conditions and a short photoperiod (time during which they receive illumination each day). But, of course, this isn't always easy, so breeders tend to breed their animals in the first few months of the season when many assume they will have better results. Keep in mind that just because your pet is sexually mature doesn't necessarily mean you should use them to breed. After showing signs that they are ready for reproduction, ideally you should wait even longer.

The energy expenditure these animals need to generate new offspring is substantial, especially females, so we should choose slightly larger and older animals for this purpose. This is not necessarily a rule with males, but it's still best to use older males. Breeding young females can even kill them. Before the start of the season, condition your amphibians with quality food, leaving them healthy and fit for the task.

Reproduction

Despite the photoperiod equation and temperature decrease, mating does not always occur by itself. You can take steps to help trigger reproduction, in other words, to demonstrate to your salamanders that it's time to reproduce.

The main step is a slight temperature change, just a few degrees; this change should be sudden enough for them to notice quickly but simultaneously slow enough so as not to stress the animals. A water temperature of 53° to 60°F is best suited for breeding. However, if you want to stimulate the laying of the eggs, reach these temperatures and increase the volume of water in the aquarium.

Keep your spawn tank in a quiet place and, as always, with stable parameters. The axolotl has sexual reproduction with internal fertilization. The axolotl is oviparous, meaning the females lay eggs. The Mexican axolotl is capable of laying anywhere from a hundred to six-hundred eggs!

In general, these salamanders follow an exciting pattern of reproduction, where they engage in a courtship ritual in which the male and female push their cloacas while making circular movements. The male then retreats, giving his rear and tail a wavy shape, but is followed by the female. Afterward, the male will vigorously flick his tail to deposit a cone-shaped gelatinous mass, which contains the sperm, and is known as a "spermatophore."

The female moves over what is deposited by the male, waving her tail and collecting the spermatophore with her cloaca. All this takes place on the substrate or some rock. Then, the following night, spawning begins, which can last until the early hours of the day. The female lays the eggs in groups of four to ten on the plants, trunks, and ornaments in the aquarium (and even on the glass). These eggs are equipped with a capsule that protects the embryo from the external environment. Ideally, you should use a separate tank for breeding your animals. Otherwise, the parents may eat the larvae.

How do I know if my axolotl is pregnant?

As axolotls are oviparous, they do not get pregnant. However, the females carry eggs in their bellies. You'll see your female with a full, swollen belly. The large belly could indicate that your female is full of eggs. Females keep the eggs for a short time in their bellies, so you will quickly have confirmation that they were real eggs in their abdomen. In up to 24 hours, she will spread the eggs throughout the aquarium, and these are very visible, so you will have all the confirmation you need. You should be prepared to see these signs; from there, prepare to welcome axolotl babies.

Egg laying

Axolotls can spawn many eggs, from fifty to fifteen hundred. The number depends on numerous factors, such as the female's age and the environment's sanitary conditions. Having decorations like plants (even if artificial) help the female when she lays her eggs. That means less stress and a healthier mother and offspring. After spawning, you must remove either the parents or the eggs from the aquarium. I recommend using a separate aquarium for reproduction, so you can remove the parents instead of the eggs.

If in good physical condition, the male can be placed with another female for mating again. The female that laid the eggs must be separated and conditioned, with good food and quality water for a few days, until she is healthy and ready for another reproduction. Females take around 12 hours to lay their eggs, which usually occurs at night, and must never be disturbed during the egg-laying ritual. You may even be alarmed at first, as the female cloaca looks swollen with a pink or red hue, but don't worry, this is normal.

The eggs are laid in clusters as they leave the female's behind in a spaced way; this helps the deposit with a movement of the hind legs. Ideally, you should observe the entire process closely. If you notice any problems or something strange has come out of the female's cloaca, immediately seek help from a specialist.

Eggs

By now, you've been taking care of the parents, and after laying the eggs, your work on reproduction begins.

You may not always want or be able to handle all these eggs and larvae. In addition, egg-laying occurs in many aquariums without the animal's owner even realizing that reproduction is in progress. There are some alternatives to address this.

Dealing with unwanted eggs

In unwanted reproduction, which usually occurs in the animals' main aquarium, the most straightforward approach is to let nature take its course. The eggs will hatch, and the parents will eat all the baby axolotls. This is undoubtedly the easiest way out of this problem. You must always remove eggs that have not hatched or have suffocated from being deprived of oxygen to avoid degrading the water quality.

Another alternative is to remove and freeze the eggs right after they're laid. The faster the eggs are frozen, the better; in this way, we avoid freezing already-formed animals. Once frozen, you can discard them. Finally, perhaps the best alternative is to sell or donate the eggs to someone who wants to keep them. It is relatively easy to find these people online in forums or on social media. Aquariums or pet stores may also accept eggs in exchange for equipment, feed, and other animals.

If you have axolotls of unknown origin, I recommend that you not breed them, let alone sell or donate their eggs. Axolotls are overproduced animals all over the world. Mass breeding has created several genetic problems, which are minimized by serious breeders, but perpetuated by amateur breeders. When you raise animals from unknown sources, you perpetuate unwanted genes. Not breeding or euthanizing the eggs and offspring is the best way to keep the population in the hobby healthy and robust.

Raising eggs

It is essential to remove the parents from the breeding tank or, if the eggs are in the main tank, remove the eggs. Do not leave the female with other males; as previously advised, take her to an isolated aquarium and recondition her. The eggs must be taken out very carefully and placed in another aquarium or container with a low water column and little aeration. Aeration is essential, as eggs in stagnant water are more likely to mold and spoil, but eggs in high water movement are also expected to fail.

If you are using the breeding tank, this should not be a problem, as long as the filter is well-sized. In containers with eggs, you should find the perfect aeration. The water in the aquarium where you transferred the eggs must have the same parameters as the aquarium where the spawning occurred. Water temperature is critical and directly determines incubation time. Many embryos cannot tolerate temperatures below 50°F; the low temperature prevents the correct nutrition of the embryo.

With temperatures above 68°F, incubation will accelerate from the usual three or four weeks to less than fifteen days. This is the average temperature I recommend. In addition to temperature, oxygenation and egg size also influence the incubation period. The most advisable lighting is fourteen hours a day, and its intensity can remain constant.

An essential factor in embryonic development is pH, which in some cases inhibits embryo formation, so the more acidic your water, the greater the mortality. As always, the higher the water exchange rate, the better the water quality and the faster and better the development of eggs and embryos. Always remember to equalize the parameters of the new water with the water taken from the container. You should already have everything you need to feed the larvae from this stage.

Egg development

The stages of development of the embryo inside the egg are easily perceived. The embryo is the darkest part inside the transparent capsule, and you can follow its development without any problems. As the developmental stages advance, you will notice a gradual change in the shape of the embryos inside the capsule. The first apparent change is that the embryo acquires a flatter shape, different from the previous circular shape. Around 68°F, this should take 3-6 days.

The next aspect you will notice is that the flattened point becomes comma-shaped, elongating, and gradually developing a visible tail and a head at the other end. From here, it is already distinctly a salamander.

From now on, around 10 to 12 days, the appendages, such as eyes and gills, will begin to develop. This is the last stage of development, the stage just before hatching. This cycle, at the temperature mentioned, should occur at around 15 days, and the larvae will now be approximately 10 mm (almost half an inch) long.

Taking care of larvae

If you separate your eggs in a container, you should pick up the larvae and transfer them to another location. Due to the small size of the larvae, the same tools for poop removal can be used, such as pipettes, siphons, or turkey basters. In this case, use a container with one liter of water for every ten newly hatched larvae.

If you are using a breeding aquarium, make sure your filter doesn't suck up the larvae. A sponge filter is perfect for this phase. Larvae are extraordinarily fragile and will not survive trauma. At this stage of life, you should still change the water daily. However, the concern with the water quality must be even greater than when they were still eggs, since now they feed and excrete a more significant amount of compounds, quickly degrading the water quality.

Remember that the water that leaves must have the same parameters as the water that enters the aquarium. Likewise, avoid fluctuations, and keep every parameter in the aquarium constant. If you use small containers, when changing water and sanitizing, it is easier to have several tubs and move the animals around than to use just one.

Larvae are sensitive to several factors, so don't be discouraged if some of them die. It's normal, and until you experience raising these animals, it takes a while to fully succeed.

Feeding larvae

Baby axolotls at birth are only about 10 millimeters long, so imagine how small their mouths are. As long as the larvae are at this tiny size, you should offer little food, as they are already feeding from the moment of hatching. If the aquarium where the larvae are is well-cycled and in good maintenance condition, it will provide the necessary food for the first two days of the animals' lives. During this time, axolotls will only feed on microorganisms in the aquarium, such as green algae and protozoa, which are their primary food during the first two days of life.

After this, you should start to feed them every day and, if possible, more than once a day, as they are voracious. To prevent them from eating their siblings, we must provide them with food in quantity and quality. If they are not fed properly, the babies will perish. I recommend using brine shrimp, daphnia nauplii, or microworms (vinegar eels) as a first food. These are easy to obtain and also to create at home, take up little space, and are highly productive. Microworms can be used mainly during the first two weeks of life of baby axolotls. Nauplii are accepted for a longer time, up to around one month of life. Then you can offer them adult daphnia or brine shrimp.

Refer to the nutrition chapter if you have any questions. The larvae must be separated according to size a few days after hatching. Although the growth is high-speed, it is also very irregular, so cannibalism can occur, and the larger ones devour the smaller ones in a short time. This is why you must provide them with enough space and places to hide in the aquarium. Larvae can congregate with adults around three or four months after hatching. At six months, the animals are active, swimming around the aquarium with great agility and lightness. And they reach adult size between one and three years.

Brine shrimp

This is a small crustacean native to North America and is the first food of many aquatic creatures bred in captivity. You can get brine shrimp in eggs or portions already sold in aquarium stores, since fish larvae use it as food. The quantities purchased are usually from adult individuals, but many people don't know that the water that comes with them is full of small nauplii, which can be sieved and also used as food.

Culturing brine shrimp

Eggs are hatched in hatchlings with salt water (15-20 grams of coarse salt per liter) and good aeration so they are in constant motion. They hatch in approximately 24 hours, and you must strain them through a fine mesh (like a handkerchief, for example). As brine shrimp are small saltwater animals, when we put them in the axolotl aquarium (which is freshwater), they die after three or four hours. Because these crustaceans die quickly, you must calculate the amount of brine shrimp to offer, because whatever is not eaten will die and pollute the water. Raising these invertebrates is not always straightforward, as they depend on absolute temperature control and salty and hard water. But it is one of the best foods to offer a baby axolotl and is extremely easy to find.

Vinegar eels

Vinegar worms are an excellent option for feeding larvae in their first days due to their small size; they are longer than newly hatched brine shrimp but thinner. They have the advantage of surviving for a long time inside the aquarium, which allows their capture by baby axolotls, even if not immediately after introduction to the aquarium.

Culturing microworms

After purchasing a starter, keep them in a glass container with 50 percent apple cider vinegar, 50 percent water, and a few pieces of apple. The creation involves very little labor - just put a starter culture in the container with this mixture and forget about it, and in a short time, the worms will multiply. The disadvantage of this culture is that this worm is small in size, making it challenging to capture. In addition, it must be "sieved" with some very fine mesh and washed while still in the mesh so the vinegar does not enter the axolotl's aquarium, which could cause changes in the pH.

Daphnia

This is a widely used food and, therefore, very well known in the aquarium world. They are also called water fleas. They are tiny crustaceans of *Daphnia pullex*, *Magna*, and *Moina sp*. They are probably the ideal food for small fish and freshwater amphibians, as *Daphnia* do not die in the aquarium and will eat microscopic food as long as they are alive. They come in sizes from barely visible to those larger than 3 mm (approximately an eighth of an inch). It is a typical food source for many fish in the wild.

Daphnia is rich in Vitamin A, calcium, and many other nutrients and proteins. They are found worldwide in small puddles, ditches, and ponds. These crustaceans thrive best where food is abundant; they filter smaller organisms from the water, and eat rotifers, algae, and infusoria. Some hobbyists consider *Daphnia* one of the best foods available. However, your best bet is to start your own culture. You can buy a breeder culture and grow it at home or collect some on your own. To keep them, they only take up a little space, like the brine shrimp, and reproduce on a large scale.

Culturing Daphnia

You can find a *Daphnia* starter culture online or at local pet stores. Live cultures are more accessible to grow than cysts (the dormant stage of a microorganism). So if you want to be successful in breeding, don't buy eggs. Instead, buy one or two bags of live *Daphnia*. You can breed *Daphnia* in 4-20-liter (1-5.3 gallon) containers or aquariums. Shallower aquariums allow better light penetration for photosynthesis by phytoplankton and provide better gas exchange between the water surface and the air. Above all, larger aquariums promote the stability of water parameters. Build two or more cultures, so if something goes wrong with one, you'll always have another.

Mosquito larvae

In spring and summer, you can quickly find these larvae in any pond or container with stagnant water with a little organic matter. You can also raise them in a controlled way in an aquarium that you do not use, which should be placed outdoors so the insects can use it to lay their eggs. But beware, if you don't control the population, your house will be filled with mosquitoes!

Other foods

There are less popular foods, like *Cyclops*, *Drosophila*, and *Paramecium* cultures, but there is no need to discuss them in any detail, since the above is more than enough and provides excellent results. When the axolotl is too large to eat the foods described, you can start feeding Tubifex, bloodworms, commercial foods, and adult foods as appropriate.

Problems with larvae and eggs

Despite all your efforts, things will often go wrong, and your larvae might die or your eggs could be stifled, meaning deprived of oxygen. But don't give up. Instead, figure out what happened and try again; that way, you can perfect the art of reproducing these animals. After all, we learn from our mistakes. The main problem with eggs is the attack of fungi or bacteria. This infection happens mainly in aquariums with poor water quality or low oxygen. In these cases, the egg will appear whitish or cloudy.

It's an easy problem to understand but not always easy to fix. But remember, most of the time, it's probably related to water chemistry. You must remove rotten eggs immediately. Otherwise, it could infect others. When we are dealing with reproduction, hygiene is essential. In the case of larvae, the main reason for death is not feeding. When many larvae are kept together, it isn't easy to see which ones are feeding and which are not, but those that do not feed will perish in a short time.

Regarding the mortality of larvae (and eggs), you should always consider the genetic aspect. Most (if not all) of the axolotls you find today in the European and North American markets are hybrid species. With commercial breeding carried out by people without in-depth knowledge of animal management, many unfavorable genetic conditions have become common, which lead to the early death of animals.

Because of this, you may find several deformed young axolotls. Euthanasia is the best option for these. In healthy individuals, I'll say again, the main deadly factor is poor water quality and poor environmental hygiene. Take care to keep the growth container or breeding and growth aquarium clean and in perfect and stable condition; this is the best way to guarantee healthy offspring and a low mortality rate.

Cannibalism

Cannibalism is prevalent among axolotls. These salamanders are non-selective predators; anything that fits in their mouths is a meal. That's why it's important never to leave axolotls together with different sizes, as the smallest will always be seen as a treat. Likewise, axolotls that do not feed appropriately on the food offered will try to eat their fellows. No matter what stage of life, these animals are greedy and will always try to feed on anything smaller that moves around them.

How often do axolotls lay eggs?

As long as the aquarium conditions are ideal and the animals are well-fed, they can produce eggs constantly, which is not ideal. As I mentioned earlier, these animals expend a lot of energy to reproduce. Laying eggs constantly causes great physiological adversity, especially to the female, so the idea is that these animals produce no more than one to two times a year.

How to keep axolotls from breeding

No technique makes these animals stop trying to reproduce. The only thing to be done is to keep males and females separate.

Information for breeders

The main thing that a beginner breeder should keep in mind is that these animals produce an incredible number of babies; of course, not all of them will reach adulthood, but it is still a large number. A standard keeper will hardly have the space and equipment to keep more than ten axolotls, much less the time to dedicate to ensure these animals stay healthy.

Again, if you don't get your animals from well-known breeders with an excellent reputation, don't breed them; if it happens accidentally, freeze the eggs. If you still want to keep the offspring, you should already know where you will sell them. As soon as you see the first signs of reproduction, contact stores, friends, and breeders who may buy or adopt the offspring of your axolotl parents.

For more experienced keepers, or those who want to delve into the world of exotic animals, buy their matrices from known breeders and study reproductive genetics and animal breeding. Keep track of your animals by lineage and everything other aspect you can, and consistently distribute this information to buyers.

Only in this way will you guarantee the quality of your genetics and breeding stock. Maintain good breeding practices, create and improve your animals in lines and always go deeper into the selection and maintenance of matrices. Educate your buyers and the entire community on how to care for these animals and how breeding without structure can have severe consequences for the hobby in the future. Also, take note of the breeding, maintenance, and shipping laws in your state and country.

Crossbreeding

The concept of crossbreeding is closely related to hybridity. That is the mixing of more than one species of the same genus. In the case of axolotls, which are included in the genus *Ambystoma*, recent studies have shown that the entire population found is hybrid. You will hardly get another pure species of *Ambystoma* to mix with your aquarium animals, as they are protected and extremely rare, and also challenging to maintain.

It is common to reproduce different colors (morphs), generating animals of other colors. But this concept is linked to genetics and animal breeding, not crossbreeding. It's nothing more than crossing animals with different skin pigments, which produce different colors or offspring where a percentage of the animals will have a standard coloring. This practice does not cause problems in the animals since it is only linked to pigmentation.

Key points when breeding

1. Try as much as possible to maintain the genetic vigor of your animals, breed only animals you can trace the lineage of, and avoid breeding siblings.
2. Know about the genetic characteristics of these animals, so you will know which colors to cross, what

the colors will be, and the percentage of individuals of a given color that will be present in the offspring.

3. If you are an inexperienced breeder, use common sense, and stick with only as many individuals as you can keep without space problems. Always keep individuals separate and healthy.

4. Remember, for reproduction and keeping these animals healthy, excellent water quality and ensuring the aquarium or tub is always clean and in perfect condition is vital.

Hopefully this chapter has provided you with all you need to breed these sweet axolotls in your home. It may not seem very easy at first, and there is a learning curve, but take heart and stay with it if you're determined to reproduce this wonderful animal.

The golden tip here is always to enlist the help of professionals or serious hobbyists. There is a lot of information on the internet, but you cannot trust all of it. But there are definitely pages, videos and forums with excellent reputations, and that's where you should take your time as you study and read about how best to care for and breed your pets.

Our last chapter involves a very controversial topic: metamorphosed axolotls.

CHAPTER 6

MORPHED AXOLOTLS

A S YOU HAVE learned so far, axolotls are aquatic and neotenic animals; even after they are adults, they still maintain the morphological characteristics of when they were young. But that's not to say they can't metamorphose into terrestrial salamanders. In this chapter, you will learn about metamorphosis, why it occurs, and how to deal with metamorphosed animals.

What is metamorphosis?

I'll start by sharing the story of my friend Christian. We met on a popular online axolotl forum. He needed help with his newly acquired axolotls, so I helped him and we ended up becoming friends. His story is interesting and certainly very common. I'm sure many have gone through this.

Christian was a longtime hobbyist, keeping tropical fish and occasionally amphibians and reptiles. One day, he was visiting a new pet store that had opened in his town, and he came across cute axolotls in a tank. He ended up in love with these beautiful animals.

Knowing he had a cycled and empty aquarium at home, he decided to acquire two of these animals, without knowing much about them.

Once home, he did some research. After reading about his new pets, he realized that his aquarium was inadequate, with a high temperature and a gravel substrate. That's when he first realized that he had been wrong to have made such an impulsive purchase. After he made the necessary modifications to the aquarium, things went well... at least for a while.

One day Christian noticed that the gills of one of his axolotls were decreasing in size, and the amphibian also seemed to be getting more slender, and lost its fin, which worried Christian and sent him to do further research. But even with a lot of research, it was still unclear what was happening and why only one of the animals was showing these symptoms. He began to monitor it closely, isolating the animal in another aquarium, and made constant measurements of the water parameters, as well as numerous water changes to make sure it was stable. But his pet continued to change its morphology.

One day he woke up and found the axolotl on the ground, without gills, fins, and thick with developed legs. That's when Christian understood what had happened: his axolotl had metamorphosed and turned into a salamander! I use this story to demonstrate how important it is to research well before purchasing an animal and how you can run into problems, no matter how uncommon they are.

Metamorphosis usually occurs when the animals are kept for a long time in poor water quality. This probably was the case with Christian's axolotl, since he didn't know if the animals had been well cared for. The natural metamorphosis into salamanders is rare, but it can happen.

Axolotls transformation can also be induced, something you should never do, as it causes suffering to the animal. Metamorphosed animals have a short lifespan, hardly exceeding two years. To induce, immoral people will inject iodine into their axolotls, a cruel and unnecessary practice that leads to the animal's death.

Researchers may induce transformation through the injection of hormones, something that must be done only in laboratories. For the axolotl to live normally, it is best for metamorphosis to occur soon after the animal reaches sexual maturity, otherwise it will have problems feeding and may even need constant hormonal supplementation.

The lesson here is that you should never try to metamorphose your axolotl. The chance of success is low, and it will likely not live a long and healthy life.

What to do if your axolotl morphs

You must be aware of the signals your axolotl is giving that it is undergoing metamorphosis. Axolotls that have turned into salamanders need different care than when they are in their aquatic form.

Recognizing the metamorphosis

The first step is to recognize that your amphibian is transitioning. Salamanders differ from axolotls in their aquatic form; they do not have gills or fins, the skin acquires a thicker appearance, and the legs are noticeably more developed. These modifications allow the animal to adapt to its new life out of the water morphologically.

During metamorphosis, use logic to make it easier for your animal to adapt to terrestrial life. Some signs are easy to see: the regression of the gills, dorsal and caudal fins, the change of the eyes as they become bulging and the appearance of eyelids, as well as the thickening of the legs. The animal's coloration also changes, even among light-skinned animals like albinos; they generally become darker and less translucent. Behavioral changes are also noticeable, such as the animal becoming more active on the surface and wanting to get out of the water. These are the main signs you should notice. Of course, you won't always notice them at the beginning of the transition, but they will be there.

Removing from the tank and providing an area to morph

Morphed axolotls have terrestrial life, so getting them out of a tank filled with water is vital. You can gradually decrease the volume of water in the tank, and in the meantime, build a terrarium or paludarium (incorporates both terrestrial and aquatic elements) with a dry part and a small puddle of water.

During the transition, it is essential to provide water so the amphibian can keep its feet on the ground and its head above the water to breathe. At this stage, the animal no longer has the same swimming power as before, so they must have easy access to the water's surface. Providing access to a dry place becomes increasingly necessary as the transition progresses. This terrarium will receive the salamander after it is fully metamorphosed. Therefore, always keep the aquarium or terrarium closed. Remember, salamanders can climb!

Monitoring the full-transitioning

After your pet is fully transitioned, isolate it in a simple aquarium. This tank should contain no substrate or decorations, just a few hiding places and something like a wet paper towel as a substrate. Metamorphosis generates great physiological stress in animals. By isolating and monitoring them for a short period - around two weeks – you'll be able to tell if they are healthy. In these cases, consulting a veterinarian is a wise course of action.

Post-morphed enclosure

After the observation period, it is time to place your salamander in the terrarium or paludarium you have set up. Tiger salamanders need a moist environment to live in and like to burrow into the substrate. Be sure to provide a substrate that holds moisture content and is easy for your pet to bury in; coconut substrate, sphagnum moss, and ABG substrate are perfect. Use a thick layer, more than four inches deep.

You can decorate the terrarium to your liking. Make sure to provide burrows and caves. The rule of using decorations and rocks larger than the size of the animal's head still applies. Use a pool area or a bowl of water; the amphibian will use it to stay hydrated and also as a bathroom. Humidity should always be above 80 percent, and temperature should be between 65° and 72°F.

Introducing food

If your salamander is healthy, it will feed easily. Offer live food two to three times a week. Earthworms, crickets, mealworms, and waxworms are nutritious and readily accepted foods. Remove from the enclosure any food that the salamander does not eat.

Document your pet's transition

Documenting the entire transition, how you handled it, and everything you did to adapt your axolotl to adulthood is not strictly necessary, but it helps others who may be going through the same thing. In addition, little is known about the metamorphosis of these amphibians and the correct management of these animals in captivity, so the more information we have, the better.

You can document through photos, videos, or notes. Taking note of the parameters of air humidity, pH and water temperature, amount of food, and animal behavior, along with everything you observe, is a great way to help unveil what is happening with these animals.

Frequently Asked Questions

Q1 Why is axolotl metamorphosis so uncommon?

These animals evolved as neotenic animals (they maintain the typical characteristics of their young form after becoming adults). This characteristic is promoted through the inhibition of thyroid-stimulating hormones. This inhibition comes from the low level of iodine that these animals eat and absorb from their environment.

Q2 Should I ever try to induce metamorphosis in my axolotl?

Absolutely NOT! Inducing your axolotl to metamorphosis is a practice that leads to animal suffering and should never be done among hobbyists.

Q3 What is the lifespan of a morphed axolotl?

A metamorphosed axolotl will hardly reach more than one year of life.

Q4 What caused my axolotl to morph?

Inadequate management and adverse environmental characteristics, such as poor water quality or extreme temperatures, can cause an axolotl to undergo metamorphosis. Or an injection of iodine or hormones.

Q5 How big do morphed axolotls get?

They usually reach the same size as adult axolotls, somewhere between five to nine inches.

Q6 How often should I feed my morphed axolotl?

Feed your salamander one to three times a week. The higher the temperature, the more they will eat.

Q7 What is the gender of my morphed axolotl?

To sexually differentiate salamanders, use the same traits for differentiating axolotls. It is easier to see in the reproductive season when females have an abdomen full of eggs and swollen cloacas.

Q8 Can morphed axolotls breed?

Yes, this can happen. But there are no reports of this happening in the home aquarium, and is unlikely.

CONCLUSION

WE HAVE COME to the end of your axolotl education, at least as far as this book is concerned. You can use it both as reading and reference material when doubts arise about maintaining your axolotls. I hope you have seen that caring for these lovely animals is not very difficult, as long as you keep an eye on a few details.

Remember, water temperature is crucial; it should always be around 60°-64°F; otherwise, your axolotls will suffer and may develop issues. You must regularly test the aquarium water to guarantee the stable maintenance of the parameters and ensure the water is of superb quality. When you keep the water at its optimal quality, you prevent your animals from becoming sick; diseases among axolotls in aquariums present themselves when environmental conditions are less than ideal.

If you have problems, remember to consult a specialized veterinarian.

Feeding axolotls is an easy task, as these animals are always hungry. Remember to only offer food about the size of the amphibian's head to prevent impaction and choking. Likewise, keep only decorations larger than the size of their heads. The same goes for the substrate, which must be non-existent, very thin, or large. Beware of overfeeding, as axolotls can become obese, which causes problems such as impactions and quickly degraded water.

If you want to breed your axolotls, do it consciously; breed only animals whose origin you know and have a plan for what to do with the dozens or hundreds of baby axolotls you will have.

Don't bring these animals home simply because you think they're cute. Axolotls demand care and special equipment like coolers. Impulsive purchases lead to unwelcome, and sometimes tragic results. Diligently research and read about the animals you want to acquire *before* you purchase them.

Finally, never try to morph your axolotls; this has severe consequences for the animal.

Now that you've read, reread, and consulted this book several times, you're ready to acquire your first axolotl. Seek out a responsible and reputable breeder in your area and visit them. If you think their animals are high quality, get one - or even more than one. But always remember to cycle your aquarium first.

If the techniques shared in this book help you, please pass them on to your friends and the axolotl keeper community. And if you enjoyed the book and the knowledge I hope I've given you, please leave a review on Amazon. Positive reviews from wonderful customers like you will help others feel confident about choosing *The Only Axolotl Care Guide You'll Ever Need*. Sharing your positive experience is vital to future axolotl keepers, and I, too, will appreciate it!

REFERENCES

Axolotl care 101: Definitive guide to the mexican walking fish. Animascorp. Retrieved September 30, 2022, from https://www.animascorp.com/axolotl-care/

Meredith Clawson Axolotl breeder, & breeder, A. (2021, January 21). *The Complete Guide to Understanding Axolotl Behavior • Fantaxies*. Fantaxies. Retrieved September 30, 2022, from https://fantaxies.com/axolotl-behavior/

Meredith Clawson Axolotl breeder, & breeder, A. (2021, March 1). *How to tell the gender of your axolotl: 5 Sexing Tips • Fantaxies*. Fantaxies. Retrieved September 30, 2022, from https://fantaxies.com/axolotl-gender/

Adam. (2021, August 15). *How to lower the temperature in an axolotl tank*. Axolotl Central. Retrieved September 30, 2022, from https://www.axolotlcentral.com/post/how-to-lower-the-temperature-in-an-axolotl-tank

Admin. (2022, August 18). *Axolotl aquarium setup - complete step-by-step guide*. Care Guides For Pet Lizards. Retrieved September 30, 2022, from https://www.lizards101.com/axolotl-aquarium-setup-complete-step-by-step-guide/

Admroot. (2020, October 30). *Axolotl metamorphosis: Why is it bad?: Exotic petquarters.* Exotic PetQuarters |. Retrieved September 30, 2022, from https://exotic-petquarters.com/axolotl-metamorphosis/

Alex. (2007, April 4). *Why do my brineshrimp not hatch.* Caudata.org: Newts and Salamanders Portal. Retrieved September 30, 2022, from https://www.caudata.org/threads/why-do-my-brineshrimp-not-hatch.10140/

AnnabeleGrey. (2021, February 19). *FYI: - notes on Columnaris infections + Volumetric Holtfreter's.* Caudata.org: Newts and Salamanders Portal. Retrieved September 30, 2022, from https://www.caudata.org/threads/notes-on-columnaris-infections-volumetric-holtfreters.70041/

Axolotl 's Shopping List Requirements And Basic Items Need To Buy (Tips & Advises For Beginners). (2021). *YouTube.* Retrieved September 30, 2022, from https://youtu.be/yEzu-cGaFOc?list=PLEM8xNJvehsJZnwdIZsPIZd-NBTP_Zvg8&t=98.

Axolotl care guide. Axolotl Central. (n.d.). Retrieved September 30, 2022, from https://www.axolotlcentral.com/axolotl-care-guide

Axolotl Care: 10 Common Mistakes. (2022). *YouTube.* Retrieved September 30, 2022, from https://youtu.be/IwXkahsHAIU.

Axolotl Nerd. (2022, August 31). *Can you have two or more axolotls in same tank?* Axolotl Nerd. Retrieved September 30, 2022, from https://axolotlnerd.com/two-more-axolotls-together/

Axolotl Nerd. (2022, September 4). *Are axolotls illegal?* Axolotl Nerd. Retrieved September 30, 2022, from https://axolotlnerd.com/axolotls-illegal/

Axolotl Nerd. (2022, September 5). *Axolotl breeding guide - how to breed axolotls in Aquariums?* Axolotl Nerd. Retrieved September 30, 2022, from https://axolotl-nerd.com/axolotl-breeding/

Axolotl Nerd. (2022, September 5). *Setting up axolotl aquarium - tank size, filter, plants, decor & more.* Axolotl Nerd. Retrieved September 30, 2022, from https://axolotlnerd.com/axolotl-aquarium-setup/

Axolotl Nerd. (2022, September 6). *Axolotl diseases, parasites & treatments.* Axolotl Nerd. Retrieved September 30, 2022, from https://axolotlnerd.com/axolotl-diseases-parasites-treatments/

Axolotl Nerd. (2022, September 6). *Axolotls feeding - the complete guide.* Axolotl Nerd. Retrieved September 30, 2022, from https://axolotlnerd.com/axolotls-feeding/

Axolotl. Minecraft Wiki. (n.d.). Retrieved September 30, 2022, from https://minecraft.fandom.com/wiki/Axolotl

Best Way: Aquarium Set-Up On A Chiller (Tagalog). (2022). *YouTube.* Retrieved September 30, 2022, from https://youtu.be/XmtPSCQo4ys.

Bringing home your axolotl - introducing to a new tank, first axolotl. Axolotl City. (n.d.). Retrieved September 30, 2022, from https://axolotlcity.com/bringing-home-your-axolotl-introducing-to-a-new-tank/

Common disease conditions in axolotls - WSAVA 2015 Congress - Vin. Powered By VIN. (n.d.). Retrieved

September 30, 2022, from https://www.vin.com/
apputil/content/defaultadv1.aspx?pId=14365&catId=
73681&id=7259254&ind=97&objTypeID=17

Cycling Guide. Axolotl Central. (n.d.). Retrieved September 30, 2022, from https://www.axolotlcentral.com/
cycling-guide

Dazkeirle. (2011, September 18). *How to create a java moss wall.* Caudata.org: Newts and Salamanders Portal. Retrieved September 30, 2022, from https://
www.caudata.org/threads/how-to-create-a-java-
moss-wall.35368/

Deep clean the Axolotl Tank with me!: axolotl updates. (2020). *YouTube.* Retrieved September 30, 2022, from https://youtu.be/ntqryVQta9w.

DingoDoo. (2012, January 16). *Question: - why do axolotls yawn?* Caudata.org: Newts and Salamanders Portal. Retrieved September 30, 2022, from https://www.
caudata.org/threads/why-do-axolotls-yawn.44801/

Evershine. (2012, May 26). *Question: - how often do axolotl lay eggs?* Caudata.org: Newts and Salamanders Portal. Retrieved September 30, 2022, from https://
www.caudata.org/threads/how-often-do-axolotl-
lay-eggs.47129/

FAQ. Axolotl Central. (n.d.). Retrieved September 30, 2022, from https://www.axolotlcentral.com/faq

Glen. (2022, September 15). *Why is my axolotl's skin peeling? [slime in axolotl tank].* Pets From Afar. Retrieved September 30, 2022, from https://petsfromafar.com/
why-is-my-axolotl-skin-peeling/

H, J. (2020, December 10). *5 weird but normal axolotl behaviors*. PetHelpful. Retrieved September 30, 2022, from https://pethelpful.com/exotic-pets/5-Weird-but-Normal-Axolotl-Behaviors

Health and Injury. AXOLITTLE AXOLOTLS. (n.d.). Retrieved September 30, 2022, from https://axolittle axolotls.weebly.com/health-and-injury.html

Herp veterinarians. (n.d.). Retrieved September 30, 2022, from http://www.anapsid.org/vets/index.html#vetlist

How To: Set Up An Axolotl Tank Hd. (2012). *YouTube*. Retrieved September 30, 2022, from https://youtu.be/_KnmQ0WxNMI.

InMemoryOfKoNa. (2016, February 25). *Question: - what are the best types of lights for an axolotl tank?* Caudata.org: Newts and Salamanders Portal. Retrieved September 30, 2022, from https://www.caudata.org/threads/what-are-the-best-types-of-lights-for-an-axolotl-tank.67215/

Is Tetra Aquasafe Safe For Axolotls? (2020). *YouTube*. Retrieved September 30, 2022, from https://youtu.be/LeWPweMDPPk?t=366.

Karma1780. (2011, December 27). *Question: - cannibalism stage*. Caudata.org: Newts and Salamanders Portal. Retrieved September 30, 2022, from https://www.caudata.org/threads/cannibalism-stage.44386/

Maillot, A. (2021, August 15). *Minecraft: Everything you need to know about Axolotls*. TheGamer. Retrieved September 30, 2022, from https://www.thegamer.com/minecraft-axolotls-facts-trivia/

Maintenance Routine (Cycled Tank) For Axolotls. (2021). *YouTube.* Retrieved September 30, 2022, from https:// youtu.be/mZtGfClXXQg.

MandiceP. (2013, April 28). *DIY/homemade hides.* Caudata. org: Newts and Salamanders Portal. Retrieved September 30, 2022, from https://www.caudata.org/ threads/diy-homemade-hides.48431/

MarieKarma1311. (2016, November 24). *What to do if your axolotl morphs.* Caudata.org: Newts and Salamanders Portal. Retrieved September 30, 2022, from https:// www.caudata.org/threads/what-to-do-if-your-axolotl-morphs.69570/

Metamorphosed Axolotls & Tiger Salamanders. Axolotls - Metamorphosed & Tiger Salamanders. (n.d.). Retrieved September 30, 2022, from https://www.axolotl.org/ tiger_salamander.htm

Monkeysniffer. (2008, August 7). *How can I tell if a axolotl is pregnant?* Caudata.org: Newts and Salamanders Portal. Retrieved September 30, 2022, from https://www.caudata.org/threads/how-can-i-tell-if-a-axolotl-is-pregnant.21842/

My Baby Dinosaur is Evolving? (Axolotl Metamorphosing). (2019). *YouTube.* Retrieved September 30, 2022, from https://youtu.be/h83XMQmgch4.

PatricALOTL. (2011, August 22). *Suitable paint for aquarium ornament.* Caudata.org: Newts and Salamanders Portal. Retrieved September 30, 2022, from https://www.caudata.org/threads/suitable-paint-for-aquarium-ornament.30225/

Prohecy. (2011, June 20). *Illness/sickness: - weird behaviour with spinning.* Caudata.org: Newts and Salamanders Portal. Retrieved September 30, 2022, from https://www.caudata.org/threads/weird-behaviour-with-spinning.39502/

Raising axolittles. AXOLITTLE AXOLOTLS. (n.d.). Retrieved September 30, 2022, from https://axolittle axolotls.weebly.com/raising-axolittles.html

Ravichandran, R., & Rajkumar RavichandranWelcome to Learn About Pet. My name is Rajkumar Ravichandran and I love all pets. (2022, April 7). *Axolotl poop : 5 clear ways to clean axie poop - 2022.* Learn About Pet. Retrieved September 30, 2022, from https://learn-aboutpet.com/axolotl-poop/

Ravichandran, R., & Rajkumar RavichandranWelcome to Learn About Pet. My name is Rajkumar Ravichandran and I love all pets. (2022, February 19). *Axolotl mouth : 9 interesting facts about axolotl mouth open.* Learn About Pet. Retrieved September 30, 2022, from https://learnaboutpet.com/axolotl-mouth/

Ravichandran, R., & Rajkumar RavichandranWelcome to Learn About Pet. My name is Rajkumar Ravichandran and I love all pets. (2022, March 3). *DIY axolotl hides : (7 interesting ideas) - 2022.* Learn About Pet. Retrieved September 30, 2022, from https://learnaboutpet.com/diy-axolotl-hides/

Robert, N. (2022, September 21). *15+ axolotl colors: Common & rare types of axolotl.* More Reptiles. Retrieved September 30, 2022, from https://www.morereptiles.com/axolotl-colors/

Robert. (2022, March 25). *Axolotl breeding.* Fishkeeping World. Retrieved September 30, 2022, from https://www.fishkeepingworld.com/axolotl-breeding/#:~:text=a%20little%20darker.-,How%20Often%20Can%20You%20Breed%20Axolotl%3F,the%20tank%20conditions%20are%20right.

Robin, R. (2011, September 18). *2 axolotls in one tank?* Caudata.org: Newts and Salamanders Portal. Retrieved September 30, 2022, from https://www.caudata.org/threads/2-axolotls-in-one-tank.42408/

Sick axolotl. (2011). *YouTube.* Retrieved September 30, 2022, from https://youtu.be/mO0AIrO-BL0.

Signs of stress and illness in axolotls. Axolotl Planet. (2022, June 27). Retrieved September 30, 2022, from https://axolotlplanet.com/axolotl-sickness-and-health/

Signs of stress and illness in axolotls. Axolotl Planet. (2022, June 27). Retrieved September 30, 2022, from https://axolotlplanet.com/axolotl-sickness-and-health/

Sordillo, S. (2022, March 28). *Why are axolotls illegal to own in some states and provinces?* Axolotl Central. Retrieved September 30, 2022, from https://www.axolotlcentral.com/post/why-are-axolotls-illegal-to-own-in-some-states-provinces

Spearman, M. L., Mark, & Mullins, L. (2022, July 3). *Axolotl tank setup - the ultimate guide.* AquariumStoreDepot. Retrieved September 30, 2022, from https://aquariumstoredepot.com/blogs/news/axolotl-tank-setup

Sunny. (2019, December 2). *Sick axolotl, fungus, stress symptoms [the definitive remedy guide].* ExoPetGuides.

Retrieved September 30, 2022, from https://exopet-guides.com/axolotl/axolotl-symptoms-guide

Sunny. (2019, December 2). *Sick axolotl, fungus, stress symptoms [the definitive remedy guide].* ExoPet-Guides. Retrieved September 30, 2022, from https://exopetguides.com/axolotl/axolotl-symptoms-guide/#test-water

Sunny. (2019, November 12). *31 interesting axolotl facts that will blow your mind.* ExoPetGuides. Retrieved September 30, 2022, from https://exopetguides.com/axolotl/axolotl-facts/

Sunny. (2020, January 10). *18 types of axolotl colors you can own (axolotl color guide).* ExoPetGuides. Retrieved September 30, 2022, from https://exopetguides.com/axolotl/axolotl-colors/

Sunny. (2021, May 13). *Axolotl care: How to take care of an axolotl.* ExoPetGuides. Retrieved September 30, 2022, from https://exopetguides.com/amphibians/axolotl-care/

Sunny. (2021, May 13). *Axolotl care: How to take care of an axolotl.* ExoPetGuides. Retrieved September 30, 2022, from https://exopetguides.com/amphibians/axolotl-care/#chapter-2

Team, E. (2021, September 17). *How much do axolotl cost?+tank and accessories.* Amphibian Life. Retrieved September 30, 2022, from https://www.amphibianlife.com/axolotl-cost/

Team, E. (2021, September 23). *How to feed worms to axolotl? A guide to worm farming!* Amphibian Life. Retrieved

September 30, 2022, from https://www.amphibian-life.com/how-to-feed-worms-to-your-axolotl/

Team, E. (2021, September 23). *How to feed worms to axolotl? A guide to worm farming!* Amphibian Life. Retrieved September 30, 2022, from https://www.amphibian-life.com/how-to-feed-worms-to-your-axolotl/

Unusualpetsguide. (2022, January 26). *Constipated axolotl? what causes it and how to treat.* Unusual Pets Guide. Retrieved September 30, 2022, from https://www.unusualpetsguide.com/2021/12/21/constipated-axolotl-what-causes-it-and-how-to-treat/

Unusualpetsguide. (2022, May 20). *Axolotl swollen throat? causes and treatment for swollen axolotl.* Unusual Pets Guide. Retrieved September 30, 2022, from https://www.unusualpetsguide.com/2021/12/15/axolotl-swollen-throat-whats-the-cause-and-how-to-treat/

Unusualpetsguide. (2022, May 20). *GUIDE ON AXOLOTL gills problems - healthy vs unhealthy (with PICS).* Unusual Pets Guide. Retrieved September 30, 2022, from https://www.unusualpetsguide.com/2022/01/12/axolotl-gills-how-to-treat-gills-problems-with-pics/

What To Do In Your Aquarium During Power Outage. (2021). *YouTube.* Retrieved September 30, 2022, from https://youtu.be/keLlK56bo78.

YouTube. (2013). *How and What To Feed Your Axolotl.* *YouTube.* Retrieved September 30, 2022, from https://www.youtube.com/watch?v=qJcJymkVS8Y.

YouTube. (2013). *How To: "Axolotless" Cycling. YouTube.* Retrieved September 30, 2022, from https://www.youtube.com/watch?v=QrfpbnaUSjY&feature=youtu.be.

YouTube. (2020). *Axolotl Decoration Do'S & Don'Ts! YouTube*. Retrieved September 30, 2022, from https://www.youtube.com/watch?t=160&v=AmMbq8ZKtsI&-feature=youtu.be.

YouTube. (2021). *Axolotl 's Shopping List Requirements And Basic Items Need To Buy (Tips & Advises For Beginners)*. *YouTube*. Retrieved September 30, 2022, from https://www.youtube.com/watch?v=yEzu-cGaFOc.

YouTube. (2021). *How To Prepare Worms To Axolotl*. *YouTube*. Retrieved September 30, 2022, from https://www.youtube.com/watch?v=S_CzXOocURk&feature=youtu.be.

YouTube. (2021). *The Differences of Minecraft Axolotls & Real Axolotls*. *YouTube*. Retrieved September 30, 2022, from https://www.youtube.com/watch?v=_-OySQPNUL4&feature=youtu.be.

YouTube. (2021). *The Truth About Morphed Axolotls*. *YouTube*. Retrieved September 30, 2022, from https://www.youtube.com/watch?v=bb3rQOcGN8o&feature=youtu.be.

YouTube. (2022). *I was Wrong about Morphed Axolotls*. *YouTube*. Retrieved September 30, 2022, from https://www.youtube.com/watch?v=B0gWyBF1zLo&t=160s.

YouTube. (2022). *Moss Wall Diy (Guide & Tutorial)*. *YouTube*. Retrieved September 30, 2022, from https://www.youtube.com/watch?v=qNUQ9ZCe0tQ&feature=youtu.be.

YouTube. (2022). *Why axolotls make Terrible pets (pls watch this before getting an axolotl)*. *YouTube*. Retrieved September 30, 2022, from https://www.youtube.com/watch?v=HSZoXZm6s2s.

Zeeman3000. (2009, February 1). *Question: - setting up aquarium chiller?* Caudata.org: Newts and Salamanders Portal. Retrieved September 30, 2022, from https://www.caudata.org/threads/setting-up-aquarium-chiller.24587/

Zronclown. (2010, September 22). *Is this normal behaviour?* Caudata.org: Newts and Salamanders Portal. Retrieved September 30, 2022, from https://www.caudata.org/threads/is-this-normal-behaviour.35070/

GLOSSARY

Minecraft: Electronic game where you build things with blocks and explore an open and free virtual world;

Ammonia: Colorless gas, formed by one nitrogen atom and three hydrogen atoms;

Bacterial disease: Term used to characterize diseases caused by pathogenic bacteria;

Black worms: Annelids of small size that present the black coloration;

Bloodworms: Larvae of an insect of the Order Diptera and belonging to the largest family of aquatic insects, the Chironomidae;

Cannibalism: When a being eats part or even the entire body of an individual of the same species;

Cloaca: Part of the intestines of birds, amphibians, reptiles, and some fish that constitutes a common chamber for the reproductive and excretory systems;

Cloudy water: Water with high turbidity;

Composting: A biological process of valorization (converting to more useful products) and recycling of organic matter in boxes where worms and microorganisms transform domestic waste generated in the kitchen and backyard into fertilizers;

Fin: External structures that many aquatic animals have to aid in swimming and balance;

Fungal disease: Term used to characterize diseases caused by pathogenic fungi;

Guill: Respiratory system of animals that breathe oxygen dissolved in water;

Hatchlings: Newborn individuals;

Java moss: Originally found in Southeast Asia, Taxiphyllum Barbieri is an aquarium plant;

Larva: Distinctive juvenile form that many animals undergo before metamorphosis into adults;

Metamorphosis: The changes that occur in the structure, in the form of the body, and even in the way of life of an animal;

Morph: Morphological alterations suffered by the same species due to genetic changes;

Neoteny: A form of paedomorphosis in which the organism reaches sexual maturity but retains juvenile or larval characters;

Quarantine: Type of imprisonment applied to a certain group of healthy individuals who may have been contaminated by the causative agent of some disease;

Red Wiggler worms: Annelids of the species Eisenia andrei;

Reverse osmosis (RO): Process of separating substances through a membrane that retains the solute;

Salamander: Name given to a group of urodelian amphibians that have an elongated body, tail, four limbs, and smooth, thin, scaleless skin;

Selective breeding: Consists of selective crosses, carried out by humans, to choose desirable morphological characteristics;

Sexual maturity: Age or stage of life at which an organism can reproduce sexually;

Substrate: Technical term to name a surface where living beings live;

Tank mates: Animals that live together with another species in an aquarium;

Trauma: Physical injury;

Tropical fish: These are fish that should be kept in heated aquariums;

Viral disease: Term used to characterize diseases caused by pathogenic viruses;

Worm cast: Earthworm humus is an organic fertilizer formed from the biological transformation of organic waste by the action of earthworms.

Made in United States
Orlando, FL
31 July 2025